Everyone in Providence has a library!

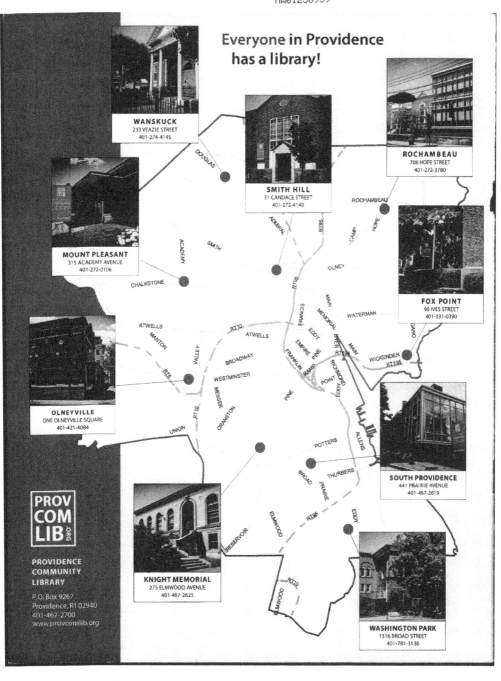

WANSKUCK
233 VEAZIE STREET
401-274-4145

SMITH HILL
31 CANDACE STREET
401-272-4140

ROCHAMBEAU
708 HOPE STREET
401-272-3780

MOUNT PLEASANT
315 ACADEMY AVENUE
401-272-0106

FOX POINT
90 IVES STREET
401-331-0390

OLNEYVILLE
ONE OLNEYVILLE SQUARE
401-421-4084

SOUTH PROVIDENCE
441 PRAIRIE AVENUE
401-467-2619

KNIGHT MEMORIAL
275 ELMWOOD AVENUE
401-467-2625

WASHINGTON PARK
1316 BROAD STREET
401-781-3136

PROV COM LIB .ORG

PROVIDENCE COMMUNITY LIBRARY

P.O. Box 9267
Providence, RI 02940
401-467-2700
www.provcomlib.org

THE FIGHT THAT SAVED
THE LIBRARIES

A TRUE RHODE ISLAND STORY

LINDA J. KUSHNER

Visit our website at **www.StillwaterPress.com** for more information.

First Stillwater River Publications Edition

ISBN: 978-1-963296-39-6

Library of Congress Control Number: 2024906036

1 2 3 4 5 6 7 8 9 10

Written by Linda J. Kushner.
Interior design by Elisha Gillette.
Published by Stillwater River Publications, West Warwick, RI, USA.

Names: Kushner, Linda J., author.
Title: The fight that saved the libraries : a true Rhode Island story / Linda
    J. Kushner.
Description: First Stillwater River Publications edition. | West Warwick,
    RI, USA : Stillwater River Publications, [2024]
Identifiers: ISBN: 978-1-963296-39-6 (paperback) | LCCN: 2024906036
Subjects: LCSH: Public libraries—Rhode Island—Providence. | Library
    finance—Rhode Island—Providence. | Regional library systems—
    Rhode Island—Providence. | Libraries and community—Rhode
    Island—Providence.
Classification: LCC: Z732.R4 K87 2024 | DDC: 027.009745—dc23

*Cover image: Kevin Veronneau, youth services specialist
with young patron at Washington Park Library.*

For the Community Libraries of Providence

"Never doubt that a small group of thoughtful, committed citizens can change the world. Indeed, it is the only thing that ever has."
　　　　　　　　　　　　　　　　　　　　　—Margaret Mead

"If you think you're too small to be effective, you have never been in bed with a mosquito."　　　　　　　　　　　　—Bette Reese

Introduction

When we were fighting to create a library system in Providence that would be responsive to community needs, many people told us that someone should write a book about the battle. It was truly a David and Goliath situation. Twenty years later, I have taken up the challenge of telling how we managed to succeed.

While the facts in this accounting are true, and the people mentioned in this memoir did actually respond to the situation as I have reported, this is a memoir and not a scholarly study. The story is told, for the most part, as I remember it, helped by interviews with many of the major players. It reflects what I remember and thought about the actions that took place. And unlike an academic writer, I have let you know how I felt about the situation as it unfolded.

The battle to keep the nine branch libraries in Providence open took five years (2004-2009) to win. At times, the challenge seemed unattainable. Our progress was delayed by the creation of endless committees, which, to my mind, were of little help in solving the problem. Each committee had to be endured and, where possible, manipulated to achieve our aims. The circularity of events, the fact that we would advert one branch closing, just to face new threats of more branches being closed, was frustrating. It may, at times, be confusing to you. But hang in. Remember, the book has a happy ending. And the fight was worth it.

Birthing a Library

I never, ever in my life thought I'd be the mother of a library system. I think it is probably the most positive thing I've done in my life, and it is exciting to see people continue to use all of the libraries.
—Linda J. Kushner, 2015

One never really knows what one will do in life. At least, that is true for me. Frequently, I seem to do things in response to a problem that needs a solution. The problems that demand my attention are not personal ones. I am lucky that my personal life seems to roll along rather smoothly, leaving me with the time and energy to devote to things beyond our family. The problems that envelop me are communal ones—usually large issues that demand governmental action and/or community organizing to fix them. My husband shudders when I clear my desk because he knows that I will get involved with an even bigger project.

The act of correcting community problems involves years of work and sometimes running for and winning political office. It involves organizing new coalitions, garnering the contributions of many people, political tact, and some luck. Suddenly, I am involved in a cadre of new issues and working with people I never knew before. These problems seem sometimes to come out of nowhere. But the reality is that the roots of the problems existed long before I decided they needed to be fixed. And so it was with creating a new library system for Providence.

The Library in Providence in 2004

IN 1964 MY HUSBAND AND I MOVED TO PROVIDENCE, A SMALL CITY OF about 100,000 people. Located in Rhode Island, the smallest and most compact state in the Union, its population of 1,000,0000 or so is ruled by six (or perhaps four) degrees of separation. Extended families, politics, churches, academic institutions, and communal activities constantly bring people into contact with each other. I soon learned it was relatively easy to affect things if one is intent on doing so. Perhaps this is because our political entities are so small. A state representative district contains 14,000 people. A Providence city councilor's district contains 12,600 souls. Six constituent letters on the same subject to a city councilor or state representative certainly catch their attention. And with the internet, Rhode Islanders are in constant contact. There are relatively few secrets in Rhode Island. Word travels quickly.

Upon arriving in Providence, I immediately got a library card for the Providence Public Library (PPL) at the branch nearest me, the Rochambeau Branch. Over the years, my family went weekly to Rochambeau, getting books for our children as they grew, and taking out novels for me and my husband to read. Occasionally, I would go downtown to the main library on Empire Street to do research in one or the other of their excellent reference collections.

I, like most library patrons, took the library for granted. We assumed that it was a part of the city government. I thought libraries, like schools, were an immutable part of city life. But that was not correct.

The Providence Public Library was a strange entity—a private corporation with a public purpose. Chartered as a private entity in 1875, PPL opened its doors in 1878. Its charter read:

> "The purpose of the corporation shall be to establish and maintain in the city of Providence a public library and such branches thereof, as may be advisable and to establish buildings for the same; to per-form and furnish library services to provide information, facilitate education, contribute to the economic and cultural development of Rhode Island, and, to advocate and promote library services in the state, so as to enrich the quality of life in Rhode Island."[1]

At first, these library services were completely supported by private

---

1 Providence Public Library Charter, Section 2. 1875.

donations. But by 1889, the library was calling on the city for aid for its libraries. The city obliged with a $7000 donation. Over the years, PPL had demanded an increasing contribution of funds from the city to provide library services. The municipal subsidy increased over the years. By 2004, the city contributed $3,000,000, which constituted 34% of the library's operating budget. The state, too, became involved in funding PPL. In 1964, recognizing that PPL's Central Library provided much-needed reference services to persons and businesses throughout the state, it started funding the State Reference Resource Center with a $100,000 contribution. This annual subsidy to the State Reference Resource Center rose over the years. In 2004, it was $880,110. In addition, the state provided annual funding for library services at PPL and for libraries throughout the state through a "grant in aid" program. For fiscal year 2004-05, the state provided $1,383,493 in grant-in-aid money to PPL. Together, the grant for the State Reference Resource Center and the grant in aid constituted 27% of the Library's operating budget. These public funds from the city and the state went to an institution that had a net worth above $56 million; over $40 million of it was in unrestricted funds.[2]

By 2004, public support (state and municipal) constituted 61% of the operating budget of PPL. Yet despite the major contribution of taxpayers to PPL, the Library continued to operate as a private institution. Its decisions were made by a private board at closed meetings with no input from the public it was designed to serve.

The Branches and Their Friend Groups

In 2004, PPL consisted of a Central library on Empire Street and nine branches in the city's diverse neighborhoods. There were

---

2 PPL's Audit Report, June 30, 2006.

three large branches—Rochambeau, Mt Pleasant, and Knight Memorial—and six smaller branches located in Fox Point, Smith Hill, South Providence, Olneyville, Wanskuck, and Washington Park.

Life in the nine branches reflected the demographics of the populations living in their catchment area. At Rochambeau, where many Russian immigrants had arrived in the 1980s and 1990s, men gathered every morning as soon as the library opened to read and discuss the news reported in the library's Russian-language newspapers. I would hear the men excitedly shouting the news across the room to each other. Their discussions became so animated that the librarians wisely decided to allocate a small closed-off room as the Russian Room. Behind closed glass doors, surrounded by Russian-language newspapers and books, the men could happily argue about the events of the day.

A continuing influx of Central and South American immigrants in the 1990s to Providence, many of whom settled in the south and west ends, created a demand for books in Spanish at the South Providence, Washington Park, and Knight Memorial branches. In the 1960s, many Hmong and other South Asian refugees, fleeing the horror of the Vietnam War and its aftermath, came to Providence. They settled primarily around St Michael's church in South Providence and on Smith Hill. The libraries in those neighborhoods responded by hanging the colorful handmade wall hangings made by the Hmong, documenting the refugees' experiences, on the walls of the libraries.

In 1999, after retiring from politics, I joined the board of the Friends of Rochambeau, an advocacy group devoted to enriching library life at the Rochambeau branch. At this time, only four of the branches had Friends Groups. The Rochambeau branch library, located on the East Side of Providence, which served a more highly educated and affluent population, was one of the first branches to establish a Friends group. Established in 1986, the Friends of Rochambeau wisely decided in 1998 to become a separate 501(c)(3) with its own tax ID number. This allowed it to control all money raised by the group.

However, the organization's sole purpose remained the enrichment of the Rochambeau branch, and the Friends group operated completely within the Library's directives.

The Rochambeau Friends had a robust fundraising operation centered around a large book sale. With these funds, the Friends underwrote passes that enabled library patrons to visit a number of museums, including, among others, the RISD Museum, the Boston Museum of Fine Arts, the Children's Museum, and the Zoo, all free of charge. It also underwrote public activities, which enriched the offerings of the branch. From time to time, the Rochambeau Friends contributed directly to PPL. In 2004, they made a $5000 donation to PPL, which at that time was in the midst of renovating the Rochambeau and South Providence branches.

In 2004, I became the President of the Rochambeau Friends. That was when I began to really learn about PPL. I was surprised to learn that PPL was suspicious of our Friends group. In fact, they were hostile to all Friends Groups. While PPL was glad to accept our financial contributions, they were antagonistic to our very existence. One of the first things I had to deal with as President was PPL administrators' refusal to allow the Friends to post notices of their activities on the bulletin boards located in the Rochambeau branch. This was ridiculous. The branch was for the enjoyment of its patrons. Besides, these notices not only advertised Friends' events like community meetings and poetry contests, but they also advertised the activities that raised the money that was used to support the library's services.

Smith Hill was a small branch, but it had one of the most vocal and feisty Friends Group. In part because it was a small branch, PPL repeatedly threatened to shut it down. In 1992, when PPL threatened to close the Smith Hill branch again, the Smith Hill Friends took PPL to court. The case ended with a settlement in Superior Court, stopping PPL from closing Smith Hill. This seemed to keep PPL at bay until 2006, when Smith Hill, along with the other small libraries, were again on the chopping block.

Part of the strength of this small library came from their librarian, Mary Jones. Ms. Jones was actually a clerk rather than a librarian, but she had such close connections with the community and was held in such high regard that she was a force to contend with. "My mother," said her daughter Althea Graves, "was a very vocal person." This was an understatement. When Ms. Jones saw a problem, she took steps to help solve it. She was a co-founder of the Smith Hill. Community Development Corporation and served on the board of the Neighborhood Health Center. With her deep ties to the neighborhood organizations, she was, of course, on a first-name basis with the area politicians.

Although "a little library," Smith Hill served a surprisingly broad swath of the city. The majority of its users were working-class homeowners who lived in the three-deckers of the neighborhoods off Smith Street. But it also served the people who lived in the housing projects in the Wanskuck area as well as patrons from the Camp Street area on the lower East Side who found the Rochambeau branch "too intimidating" and preferred the "hominess" of Smith Hill.[1]

Whereas the strength of Rochambeau Friends was that it was an independent 501©(3) and that the branch library served a wealthy, more educated section of the city, the strength of Smith Hill was in its close ties to the community. Under the guidance of Mary Jones, it became known as a welcoming community center where one could find warm advice and even help with personal problems as well as books.

Mount Pleasant, another large branch, also had a Friends Group. This Friends Group, founded in 1981 like the Rochambeau branch, offered many enrichment programs for Mount Pleasant patrons. But it had less financial independence. Any funds the Mount Pleasant Friends raised were kept by PPL in a separate account for Friends Groups. It was dependent on PPL for the maintenance and disbursement of its

---

1 Personal interview with Althea Graves, January 12, 2023

funds. Maureen Romans, an adjunct professor of political science at Rhode Island College, was the president of the Mt. Pleasant Friends.

A fourth Friends Group was started in 2003 at Fox Point Library, a small branch located near Brown University in two basement rooms of the local Boys' Club. The branch users included many highly educated people, and the library had active adult patronage. The creation of the Fox Point Friends alarmed PPL. They immediately drafted a plan of what the Fox Point Friends could and could not do. The plan stated that all the projects of the Friends group were to be chosen by the librarian; all statements made to the city council must be in support of PPL policies; and all money raised by the Friends Group must be turned in to PPL each year.[2] This admonition by PPL seemed to have little effect on the actions of the newly founded Fox Point Friends Group. In 2004, Sheri Griffin, a member of the Friends Group, circulated a city-wide petition calling for reform of the Library.

PPL seemed to be antagonistic to the formation of any new Friends Group. In the summer of 2005, when patrons of the Central Library tried to create a Friends Group in response to PPL's decision to create the "Empire Branch" located within the Central Library, the administration came down on them like a ton of bricks. And after a few months, the Central Branch Friends Group, ambitiously named FOPPL (Friends of Providence Public Library), came to an ignominious end.

Precipitating Actions of 2004

ALTHOUGH THERE SEEMED ALWAYS TO HAVE BEEN TENSION BETWEEN PPL and the city, the spring of 2004 was particularly bad. The previous

---

2 Minutes of the Friends of Rochambeau, President's report. January 3, 2005.

spring, PPL had threatened to reduce library services if the city did not increase its annual contribution to PPL by $1.5 million. The city, however, facing its own economic problems, decided to continue to fund the Library at the $3 million level. They did, however, provide an additional $350,000 worth of books for the Library in the city's master lease. The Library also received an additional $655,000 from the state by virtue of newly enacted state legislation that allowed the state to match a proportion of the money that a library contributed to operations from its endowment. This money was in addition to the state funds PPL received under the grant-in-aid program and the grant for the support of the State Reference Resource Center.

In June of 2004, PPL librarians learned that the Library administration was considering reducing the staff by sixty people, forty at the Central Library and twenty at the branches. In addition, library hours would be reduced. They also learned of plans to close the Central Library's Washington Street entrance and to reopen the Library's entry on Empire Street, which had been closed since 1987. The door shifting was part of a large renovation connected to creating a "branch library" within the Central Library. These changes would cost $200,000. The creation of a branch library at Central was a ploy to divert city aid to support the operation of the Central Library since the city's contribution was customarily used to support branch operations.[1]

---

1 Arguing that the branches served city residents, PPL had developed the practice of allocating any direct cost involved in running the branches (as well as a portion of indirect costs of the administration of PPL (e.g. the cost of administration, tech services and IT) as expenses to be paid only with City money. By creating a new "branch" at the Central Library they were able to shift the costs of running the children and popular library departments located at the downtown library to the city. "All of the funding from the City of Providence and state grant-in aid program will be used to support the operating expenses of our branch library system...All of the State funding for the Statewide Reference Resource

"Marches Up Washington Street", Providence Journal,
March 2006, Glenn Osmundson, photographer

By July, PPL had eliminated twenty-one librarians and fourteen clerical workers (sixteen of whom took voluntary leave). The hours at the Central Library were reduced from sixty-one to forty-eight hours a week, eliminating most weekday evening hours and all Saturday hours. Library hours at the branches were also cut by fifty-four hours per week. The larger libraries were now open only forty-five hours a week, the smaller ones only thirty and ½ hours per week.

In August, PPL laid off seven custodial workers—who were members of the United Service and Allied Workers of Rhode Island—and outsourced their job of cleaning the libraries to two private cleaning

---

Center, which by state law operated at the Central Library, will go to supporting this state service." Letter from Dale Thompson to Mr. and Mrs Harold Kushner dated July 27, 2004, in author's possession.

"Demonstration in Front of City Hall", Providence Journal, May 2006

companies. The custodian workers promptly appealed this action to the National Labor Relations Board.

The public's response to PPL's cuts and layoffs was immediate and fierce. It was fueled in part by the knowledge—learned from IRS filings—that, while crying poverty, PPL from 1998 and 2002 had increased the top five administrator's salaries by roughly twelve percent a year. Library Director Dale Thompson was now paid $132,957. This was more than either the governor of Rhode Island or the mayor of Providence earned.[1] Her salary was also significantly higher than the salaries of other public library directors in cities of comparable size in other states.

The first to respond to the administration's announcement of

---

1 Karen Lee Ziner, "Library workers lash out over executives' raises'" *Providence Journal* (June 24, 2005).

the layoffs and costly remodeling plans for the Central Library were the librarians themselves. Learning of the planned changes at a staff meeting in May, they formed a group called "Library Defense" and immediately sent out hundreds of letters, some signed and some anonymous, detailing the actions of PPL. These letters careened around the internet, alerting the outside world and the press to what was happening at PPL. Their website, www.prolibdefense.org., which informed the public of what was going on at PPL, collected support from librarians across the country. The past president of the American Library Association wrote from New York to urge the librarians to "organize your colleagues and the citizens of Providence to fight back to save library services." A letter signed by Elizabeth G. Johnson, an information-service Librarian at Cranston Public Library, and thirty-two former librarians at PPL, published in the Providence Journal on July 11th, disputed PPL's claim that the cuts were made because the Library lacked adequate funds to fully staff the Library. Their letter listed the money the Library received from the city and the state through various grants and the fact that PPL had over $35,000,000 in unrestricted funds. It was an eye-opener for the reading public, including, I am sure, members of the Providence City Council.

Notwithstanding PPL's admonishment to the Fox Point Friends not to criticize PPL, the fledgling organization immediately started a petition protesting the cuts. The petition spread throughout the city. By July 8th, the organizers were able to present 2000 signatures to the library administrators. The petition asked library administrators "to withdraw their current plan for restructuring the library system and to hold a public meeting at which they can explain their rationale and take questions and comments from the audience."

I knew immediately that the actions of the PPL Board would not only affect service at Central, but these actions also threatened the branches. Library service at the branches had always been of secondary importance to PPL. In the case of the smaller branches, it was of tertiary concern to the Board, which concentrated its attention on the "flagship" Central Library.

Like hundreds of others, I wrote a letter complaining to Dale Thompson about the proposed actions. Like all the others, I received no response. Maybe arrogantly, I was amazed that she did not respond to me. After all, I was the president of the largest Friends Group, and our Friends group had actually contributed funds to PPL. My husband and I were also donors to PPL. And Rochambeau, the branch I represented, was the home library of many of PPL's largest donors. Obviously, this did not count.

The dismissiveness of PPL's administrators was backed up by its board. As the President of the Rochambeau Friends, I wrote to Joel Stark, the president of the PPL Board and to about twenty other board members in March 2004, describing the situation at Rochambeau and suggesting a meeting. I received no answer. I again tried to set up a meeting with Joel Stark in September. This time, after the decimation at Central, I wrote to ask that the Friends Groups be represented on the Board. "I have learned that there are four vacancies on the PPL board. I would suggest that those seats be designated as seats for representatives from the Friends Groups in the city. If PPL is going to concentrate on being a collection of branches, they should at least have input on the board level from people who are central to the use and development of the branches." Needless to say, I was again blown off. Clearly, one needed to go public to get any response from PPL. And that is what we did.

Anger at PPL's staff cuts and its wasteful plans to change the structure of the downtown library was coming to a head. On July 9, 2004, Maureen Romans and I joined a demonstration of about 200 people in front of the library. The crowd had marched up Washington Street from City Hall to Empire Street, where they rallied in front of the Empire Street entrance to the library. A small woman, who I did not know, was wielding a bullhorn and haranguing the crowd. That woman was Patricia Raub, a history professor who specialized in

Rhode Island history. She taught courses at Rhode Island College and the University of Massachusetts and regularly used the Central Library for her research. She was alarmed by the cuts that were decimating service at the State Resource Center at the Central Library. To my knowledge, Patricia Raub had never led a public movement, but the actions of PPL had enraged her.

I think of the meeting of Patricia and myself on Empire Street as the moment that led to the creation of the Providence Community Library (PCL) five years later. But of course, we had no idea that our struggle to get PPL to respond to the public needs would ultimately lead to the creation of a new library system for Providence.

Unbeknownst to me, another person at that rally who would play a major role in shaping PCL was Karen McAninch, the union representative of the custodial workers at PPL. Karen had learned of the rally ahead of time when she got a call from a stranger, Patricia Raub. The stranger told her about the rally and asked her if she had a bullhorn. Patricia had assumed that as a union organizer, Karen would certainly have a bullhorn. Actually, Karen did not have a bullhorn, but deciding that the rally was a good idea, she personally bought one and presented it to Patricia to use at the rally.

Creation of the Library Reform Group

AFTER OUR MEETING AT THE RALLY, PATRICIA AND I DECIDED THAT there needed to be a permanent group to coordinate all the efforts that were being made to make PPL more responsive. There was some question about how the group should be constituted. I had hoped that each Friends Group would formally designate a representative to the group. I approached the Rochambeau Friends Board about joining with representatives of other Friends Groups to work collectively for reform. Although a number of board members seemed interested, my proposal was vehemently shot down by our Treasurer, who I remember exclaimed, "Oh no, we don't want to get involved with politics!" It turned out that whether "we" wanted to or not, politics was going to be the only way to keep all the branches open. We ended up bringing together a group of people, each of whom lived in and were patrons of the separate branches. We reasoned that each person would bring the knowledge of their branch as well as their own unique experiences and expertise to the meetings.

Initially, the group was known as the Association of Friends of the Library, but when we learned that another organization was already using that name, we changed our name to the Library Reform Group, a shorter name that aptly described what we were about! Starting at the end of the summer of 2004, the group met monthly in my living room on the East Side. Patricia was its chairperson and became our spokesperson.

The neat thing about Patricia Raub and myself was that we brought different talents to the problem. Patricia was a historian and brought that perspective. She immediately established that the crisis at PPL was not new. The cuts in service threatened by PPL were just the latest iteration for branch closings. A number of similar threats, including the closure of branches, had been narrowly averted in the past twenty years. In June 2005, she and Elaine Heebner, another member of the reform group, published "Unsettled Accounts: A Brief History of the Financial Relationship between Providence Public Library and Its Public Donors." This report documented that the City/PPL problems stretched back to 1889, a few years after its founding as a private corporation, when it began to use city funds to augment its private contributions.

As a lawyer who had served six terms in the General Assembly from 1982–1994, I brought legal knowledge and political experience to the effort. I still maintained connections with many of the people who were in office. Also, because I had been the Democratic candidate for the United States Senate in 1994, my name still had some recognition across the state. This was convenient and helpful.

From the start, the Library Reform Group's major actors included patrons of the different branches in the city. Patricia lived in the Wanskuck district on the northeast side of town. She was also a regular patron of the Central Library. Maureen Romans was the president of the Mt. Pleasant Friends. I was the president of Rochambeau Friends. Also from Rochambeau was Lisa Niebels, the secretary of the Rochambeau Friends, who joined us notwithstanding the reluctance of the Rochambeau Friends to formally join. Althea Graves, the President of the Smith Hill Friends, came with her mother, Mary Jones, who was the legendary librarian at the Smith Hill branch. Sheri Griffin, who joined us for our initial meetings, was on the board of the Fox Point Friends. Rick Robbins, the co-founder of the newly founded short-lived Friends group at Central (friends of PPL or FOPPL for short), represented downtown.

Elaine Heebner brought the valuable experience of being both a native of Providence and a former employee of PPL to our group. Elaine, who regularly used the Central Library, had been the coordinator of volunteers for PPL from 1984 to 1993. She was an avid networker and researcher. Unlike many of us, she knew from the start that PPL could do whatever it wanted with the branches because it was a private institution. She had learned this as a child living in Fox Point when "her" branch library was suddenly and unceremoniously eliminated. When her mother complained about the closure, she was informed that library users had no voice in branch operations. Also, from the start, our group had the input, from time to time, of a PPL employee, our own "deep throat," so to speak.

The only branches not "represented" at the start of the Library Reform Group were South Providence, Knight Memorial, and Washington Park. But early in 2005, Rochelle Lee, a community activist in South Providence, and Deb Schimberg, a patron of Knight Memorial, joined us. In 2006, with the closing of her library in Washington Park, a fired-up Ellen Schwartz became part of the group.

From time to time, Rochelle Lee and Deb Schimberg would

identify themselves to the press as leaders of "Save our Libraries." I was surprised when I went to write this book that I couldn't remember that group having any meetings. "Oh well," explained Rochelle, the seasoned community operator, "we used the title to express the urgency of our effort. It connected with people, and it made the reform movement look bigger."[1] Marcus Mitchell, who would become a central member in the creation of the Providence Community Library, joined the reform effort in late 2007.

Understanding the Structure
of Providence Public Library

OUR FIRST PROBLEM WAS DISCOVERING WHAT THE PROVIDENCE PUBLIC Library actually was and how it functioned. It was shocking to think that even though I was the president of a Friends group and a lawyer, I had no idea about how PPL worked or even where and when they met. I had assumed they were part of the municipal government, but it seemed they were a private corporation and as such operated almost as a secret society.

I took myself to the Reference Center in the Central Library to see if they had a copy of the charter creating the library as well as a copy of its corporate by-laws. It felt strange entering into the bowels of "the enemy." I had been such a persistent and noisy critic of PPL that I knew I was a persona non grata—at least in the eyes of the Director and Chairman of the Board. I expected to be barred from seeing PPL records, but of course, the reference librarian, a true professional, helped me find the documents.

I learned from the By-laws of the Corporation that the corporation's

---

1 Interview of Rochelle Lee, December 6, 2022.

annual meeting was to be held on the first Friday in October.[2] Regular meetings of the board of trustees were held at noon on the third Thursday of each month in the Trustee's Room at the Central Library. Of course, because PPL was a private corporation, only the annual meeting was open to the public, and then only if you could find out when and where the meeting was held.

The Board itself was to be composed of between thirteen and thirty-three members of the corporation elected by the Corporation. (I could never find out how one became a member of the Corporation, but I suspected it followed the 19th-century club practices of being invited to become a member by another member). Board members could serve for life or until resignation or removal. The Charter provided that the governor and the mayor, through their representatives, could be ex-officio members of the board.

Patricia and I became, if not joined at the hip, certainly paired through the internet. Almost daily, we would exchange drafts of articles, letters, and op-eds that we were writing to make sure they were not only passionate and factual but also spelled correctly. Frequently, I would send off the first draft to Patricia with the admonition, "Do your magic," and it would come back not only with new additions but with my overlooked typos and spelling bloopers magically corrected.

Op-eds in the Providence Journal (the ProJo) offered an important vehicle to get the news out to the community. In 2004, Providence was a one-paper town. Getting an op-ed into the ProJo was difficult under any circumstances. However, an editorial critical of the Providence Public Library was even harder to publish since the ProJo was controlled by some of the same people as the Providence Public Library. Joel Stark, the chairman of the PPL Board of Trustees in 2004, had been the Senior Vice President of Marketing and Development

2 Providence Public Library Charter, By-Laws and Charter revised 1994.

at the ProJo for twenty-nine years, ending in 2001. Board member Kimberly Sutton was the wife of Howard Sutton, who was the paper's publisher and chief executive officer until his retirement in 2014. Even the editorial page editor of the ProJo, Bob Whitcomb, was a member of the PPL board. (Although, in truth, Bob rarely attended board meetings). And most significantly, the Providence Journal was one of the Library's largest donors. In 2003, it had contributed $100,000 to PPL. It was, therefore, surprising and admirable to me that the ProJo actually published our op-eds since they clearly supported the position of the Library's administration in the early years of our fight.

On June 26, 2004, a Providence Journal editorial berated the State and City for not giving PPL more money.[1] On June 27, 2004, the ProJo published a long article by Dale Thompson, the PPL director, justifying the Library's actions. Again, on December 5, 2004, Dale Thompson was given more space on the editorial pages to boast of her management of the PPL.[2]

But we got space, too. One of Patricia's first actions had been to fire off an op-ed on July 2, 2004, deploring the proposed changes at the Central library.[3] "The notion that the library would seek to de-emphasize its specialized holdings and function in favor of focusing on a popular-title collection seems indeed to be a 'dumbing down' of the library's mission," she wrote. As a scholar of Providence's architecture, she also noted that it was foolish to close the grand Washington Street entrance just at the time the city was trying to revive its downtown. "The (19th century) architecture of the library, she wrote, was meant to convey a sense of the city's wealth and influence."

---

1 Editorial, "Help is overdue for public library," *Providence Journal* (June 26, 2004)

2 Dale Thompson, "Renovating and restructuring,"*Providence Journal* (June 27, 2004).

3 Patricia Raub Editorial, "Don't dumb down Providence Public Library," *Providence Journal* (July 2, 2004).

I penned my first op-ed on Nov. 7, 2004, after attending my first PPL annual meeting:

"I attended the annual meeting of the Providence Public Library (PPL) Corporation this year," I wrote, "and I felt like I was standing on the decks of the Titanic. On the surface, the waters were calm. Administrators met us with smiles. We were taken on guided tours of the renovations the PPL Board has embarked on to reopen the Empire Street entrance, creating a separate "branch library" downtown. We sat and listened to a self-congratulatory pro-forma meeting where committee reports were accepted without a single question or comment from board members.

At no time would a listener imagine that the Providence Public Library is being systematically dismantled by a small group of people. As on the Titanic, while the band played above, disaster is taking place below deck. PPL board decisions this past year, made in private with no public input, have resulted in decimating the reference capacity of the library…. To my mind, a library is composed of books, librarians, buildings, and administrators— in that order.

This board seems to have a reverse order. Its first priority seems to be buildings…. It casts off the responsibility for funding the operation of the downtown library as it creates a superfluous "branch" on Empire Street. It raises the salaries of top administrators at the same time that it lays off library workers and custodians…. It is time for the public to step in and demand real changes in how library decisions are made before the Providence Public Library sinks any further."[4]

The Library Reform Group met regularly at my house since

---

4   Linda Kushner Editorial, "Public must step into PPL crisis," *Providence Journal* (November 7, 2004).

its start in 2004. Between the meetings, Patricia and I hammered out proposals for restructuring the PPL board, letters to political leaders, and press releases. We thought that the representatives of the major funding agencies (i.e., the city and the state) should be voting members of the PPL board. And that it should also include users of branches and the Central Library.

Gaining Traction

IT WAS CLEAR THAT IF WE WERE TO GET ANY CHANGES AT PPL, IT would have to come through pressuring the city to demand change. The Library Reform Group initiated a letter-writing campaign to the Providence City Council urging representation of branch patrons on the Library board. By early 2005, more than 350 postcards had been sent to members of the city council asking both for open meetings and for significant representation on the Board.

Although PPL seemed impervious to our protests, the city was more responsive. At the end of 2005, the mayor appointed Joseph Fernandez to represent him on the PPL board. Prior to that, the ex-officio appointments of both the mayor and the governor had been left vacant. Joe proved a welcome voice for the people. He actually questioned some of PPL's policies and voted to protect the branches. That gave us one vote on the board. Over the summer, the Library Reform Group worked to get a second vote. We sent the governor a series of letters asking him to appoint a representative to represent him on the PPL board. But he failed to act. Finally, after Patricia and I went to the Statehouse and met with David Trembly, who was on the governor's staff (and who also was a member of the Friends of Rochambeau Board), the governor made his appointment. Mark McKenney, a lawyer who had served as the chair of the Library Board of Rhode Island, joined the PPL Board as the governor's representative on Jan. 10, 2006. These two men, Joe and Mark, became voices for the public, raising cogent objections to the Library's apparent plan to dismantle the branches.

With so many letters to the editor protesting PPL's actions appearing in the ProJo and other smaller newspapers, the rallies taking place in the streets of Providence, the postcards arriving daily at the City Council's office, and the 2000 signature petition to library administrators which complained about the lack of public input in library decisions, the City Council sat up and took notice. In July, the Council mandated that the Library's subsidy would now be payable in four installments and would be contingent on PPL reporting on its use of the money before each payment.

At the September meeting of the Finance Committee of the City Council, members proposed to Joel Stark, the Chairman of the Trustees, and Dale Thompson, the Library's director, that public members be added to the Board, that the Board meet in public, and that the minutes of the meetings be disclosed. Joel Stark, of course, was non-committal.[1]

Passing the Open Meetings Law

IT SEEMED PREPOSTEROUS THAT AN ORGANIZATION WITH A PUBLIC purpose that affected a critical part of the community and that received more than fifty percent of its operating budget from public taxes could operate in complete secrecy with no public input. All other entities that used public money were open to public scrutiny through the State's Open Records Law. Drawing on my experience as a legislator, I thought we might be able to open PPL's meetings by bringing them under the Open Records law, which governs the meetings of all state and municipal entities. I approached my state

---

1   Gregory Smith, "Council asks library board to open books," *Providence Journal* (September 28, 2004).

representatives, Senator Rhoda Perry, a close personal friend, and State Representative Gordon Fox, who happened to be the Speaker of the House, about introducing a bill to open up the meetings of PPL to public scrutiny. Both of them, strong supporters of libraries, were enthusiastic about placing the Library under the mandates of the State's Open Meetings Law.

On Feb. 3, 2005, open meetings legislation was introduced in both the House and Senate.[1] The bills simply added "any library that funded a majority of its operational budget in the prior budget year with public funds" to the purview of the state's open meeting law, which already applied to all state and municipal meetings. If passed, PPL would be required to publicize the time, location, and agenda of its meetings, allow the public to attend, allow for some public comment at the end of each meeting, and post the minutes of the meeting with the Secretary of State. The bill specifically exempted "discussion of personal finances of a prospective donor to a library" from the requirement of being public. Early in March 2005, I testified before the House and Senate judiciary committees. Aware of PPL's actions of reducing library services, the House and Senate committees were very receptive. It did not hurt our effort that the Rhode Island Constitution, in Article XII, Section 1, "Duty on the General Assembly to Schools and Libraries," charges the State to "adopt all means which it may deem necessary and proper to secure to the people the advantages and opportunities of education and public library service."[2] The bill passed in June and took effect Sept 1, 2005.

Upon its passage, PPL immediately moved to shield its financial transactions from public scrutiny. On July 25th, the Board voted to set up a separate corporation, the Providence Public Library Foundation,

1 2005-H 5170; 2005 -S0242

2 Rhode Island Constitution, Article XII, Section 1, "Duty on the General Assembly to Schools and Libraries,"

which would not be subject to the open meetings law.[3] Corporate papers were filed on August 2nd for the new corporation which was governed by the same Board members officers as PPL.[4] On Sept. 5, 2005, approximately $36,000,000 of the Library's funds were transferred into this account.[5] On Sept 13th, the Board unanimously approved the transfer of its investment account and holding accounts to the Providence Public Library Foundation.

Unionizing PPL

IN SEPTEMBER, THREE MONTHS AFTER LAYING off THIRTY PERMANENT clerks and librarians, PPL hired temporary workers to perform some of the work of the dismissed staff. The remaining permanent staff found themselves in the ignominious position of having to train the temps to perform the work of their fired colleagues. After that, it was a small wonder that the staff began to consider unionizing.

The custodial workers at PPL were already represented by Karen McAninch. A seasoned union organizer, Karen had left the Service Employees International (SEIU Local 134) in 2003 to help form a new union, the United Service and Allied Workers of Rhode Island (USAW-RI). In May 2005, the USAW launched a card signing drive to become the representative of the clerks and librarians who were still at PPL. As Karen later explained to me, this was a very vulnerable time

---

3 Cathleen Crowley, "Library board seeks change," Providence Journal (August 24, 2005).

4 Cathleen Crowley, "Library board seeks change," Providence Journal (August 24, 2005).

5 According to the Providence Public Library and Providence Public Library Foundation Financial Statement, June 30, 2005 (with Independent Auditor Report there on), the value of the Foundation on June 30, 2006 was $37,806,838.

"Councilmen at City Hall Rally", Providence Journal,
May 2005, Ruben W. Perez, photographer

for the young union when other unions could raid its membership. The Union drive had the support of the Library Reform Group as well as at least seven of the fifteen City Council members. On May 19th, at a well-publicized rally at City Hall in support of unionizing the Library staff, a number of City Council members spoke up in support of the union campaign. We Library Reformers were there to cheer them on. Our presence at the rally not only provided support for the union but also boosted our relations with many City Council members. PPL lawyered up in an attempt to defeat unionization, but on Sept. 8th, fifty-three (of the hundred staff members eligible to vote) voted for the union. Thirty-nine staff members opposed it. PPL library workers were now unionized. The library workers were one of the first groups to join the fledgling USAW-RI.

On Sept. 13, 2005, as a result of the passage of the open meeting law, we were finally able to attend and comment at a PPL board meeting. The fact that we could attend the meeting was a newsworthy event. A Providence Journal article described how a security guard had to unlock a special elevator so we could ride to the third floor and enter the Trustees' Room. The meeting, it reported, "was conducted with an abundance of caution."[1] A lawyer hired by the Board was on hand to make sure that everyone abided by the Open Meetings Law.

Only a dozen of us members of the public attended. We were on hand to see the Board pass, without a discussion, a motion transferring the Library's $36,000,000 of savings and endowment to a private foundation that would shield it from public scrutiny. The meeting concluded with fifteen minutes allotted to public comments. No speaker was allowed to speak longer than two minutes. I used my two minutes to thank the Board for the opportunity to comment and to point out that the treasurer's report did not mention a single figure. I also asked that some of the savings be used for branch activity. The Board sat stoically as we made our two-minute comments. No one responded.

And what did the PPL Board look like in 2005? This meeting, as well as most board meetings, was attended by roughly twelve-sixteen of the twenty-seven voting Trustees. The impression one had was that of a white guys' meeting. There was one African American, James Vincent from Cranston, who regularly attended the meetings. Usually, two or three of the trustees present were women. The rest of the Trustees in attendance were white men.

The governance of PPL did not reflect the ethnic mix of the city. A 2003 report on Providence's population found that 42.3% were White, 35.7% were Hispanic, 17% were Black, and 5.5% were Asian. The Board roster identified six members as African American. But of these, only Jim Vincent regularly attended board meetings. Three people were identified as Hispanic and two as Asian, but I don't remember seeing them at the Board meetings I attended. This was especially disturbing when one realized that only Rochambeau was

---

1 Cathleen F. Crowley, "Public library opens meetings for the first time," *Providence Journal,* Sept 14, 2005.

located in a majority-white community. All the other branches were located in communities composed mostly of people of color with large immigrant communities. The board's actions suggested that they had little interest or experience in servicing these communities.

When the Library Reform Group examined the Board of Trustees membership list for 2004-2005, we found it listed twenty-eight voting members. Only twelve of these members lived in Providence. (At least seven of these Trustees lived on the East Side, the more affluent part of the city served by the Rochambeau branch.)

The fact that the Library was being directed by people, the majority of whom lived outside of Providence or on the East Side of Providence and who most likely had little familiarity with most, if not all, of the branches, really disturbed us. It also disturbed Mark McKenney, the governor's representative. At one Board meeting, he later recalled that when the Board was again ready to close the branches in the less affluent neighborhoods of Providence, he told his colleagues, "It is easy for you to vote to close a branch sitting here on Empire Street. But you do not know the branch, the neighborhood, or how the community values its library."[1]

The administration of PPL brushed off the criticism that many Board members did not know or use the Library. But PPL suspended a worker for three days without pay when he discovered and posted on an internal staff site that few of the members appointed by PPL to a PPL commission to deal with the future of the library actually had PPL library cards. And that fewer of those actually used them.[2]

Attending PPL board meetings became a monthly ritual for us.

---

1 Interview of Mark McKenney, 2015. StoryCorps collection, Community Libraries of Providence.
2 Cathleen F. Crowley, "Library clerk suspended for critical Web note,"*Providence Journal* (January 31, 2006. The employee subsequently received back pay for the three-day suspension after the union grieved his case. Cathleen F. Crowley, "Library settles grievance with censured employee," *Providence Journal* (March 31, 2006).

Because they were held in the morning, many reformers who had jobs with fixed hours couldn't attend. But I was always there along with Maureen Romans and Patricia Raub when she could, Elaine Heebner, Lisa Niebel, and others from the Library Reform Group. Karen McAninch, the Union Representative of PPL's maintenance workers, who also represented the library workers at Brown University, was at every meeting. She took meticulous notes and was a font of information for us about how libraries worked in general and about what was actually happening at PPL.

Another observer was Deb Furia, a PPL employee. Deb told me that before the meetings had been opened, only one PPL employee had been allowed to observe the meetings and that employee had to submit her notes of the meeting to Dale Thompson, the Library director, before they could be disseminated to other employees. Deb was not about to let the Board slip out from under the mandates of the open meetings law. One day, noting a suspicious gathering of board members meeting in the back parking lot, she took it upon herself to inquire what was happening. "Oh, they were just discussing their vacations," they told her.[3] However, her action let management know they could not shirk the mandate with impunity. Deb was at every board meeting.

Board meetings were rather cut and dry. The library director, Dale Thompson, dressed in a cashmere sweater with pearls at her neck—a model of composure—reported the activities of the library to the Board. There was little questioning by the Board. Committee reports and motions were presented, and, except for questions from Joe Fernandez, representing the mayor, and Mark McKenney, representing the governor, they passed with little discussion.

I felt quite at ease, even cocky, being there. I relished the thought that it was our work at the General Assembly that had forced them to let us in. I later learned that my compatriot, Maureen Romans, felt less at ease. An associate professor of Political Science, Maureen's

---

3   Interview of Deb Furia, May 3, 2023.

daughter Jennifer was employed at the Smith Hill branch as a children's specialist. She later told me that she felt that many of Dale's statements were directed at her personally and were threats against her daughter's job. Maureen was not just imagining that Dale had her eye on her. Jennifer later told me, when I interviewed her for this book, that Maureen Sheridan, Dale's assistant, had called and told her to "Get her mother under control."[1]

Dale's threat to fire the child specialists became explicit in 2006. Maureen remembered that Dale smirked at her as she announced that the children's specialist would be let go. A woman of action, Maureen immediately enlisted the help of her State Representative, Joanne Giannini. The State Representative was particularly concerned that the branches remain open during the after-school hours from 4:00 pm to 7:00 pm, the time when kids tended to get into trouble and needed help with their homework. Giannini warned Dale that if she went through with the cuts, she would work at the General Assembly to reduce state aid to PPL. The plan to cut the child specialists was abandoned at this time.[2] Being able to attend board meetings and see what was in the works, along with the intimacy of Rhode Island when your state Representative lived a few blocks away, allowed us to avert this threat to library services. However, PPL used the issue of eliminating child specialists again in 2007 and 2008 to strong-arm the City into giving it more money.

Working With the City

WHILE WAITING FOR THE OPEN MEETINGS BILLS TO WORK THEIR WAY through the General Assembly and become law, we tried to change

---

1 Personal Interview of Jennifer Roman, Sept 13, 2023.
2 Personal Interview of Maureen Roman, October 24, 2022.

the structure of the PPL Board by harnessing the power of the city. We were aided in this effort by the fact that Providence is such a small place. I had spent twelve years in the Legislature and was on familiar terms with many people in government. David Cicilline, the Mayor of Providence, lived in the state representative district I had represented, and he had succeeded me as its Representative when I didn't run for re-election in 1994. We had a close relationship of mutual respect.

In May 2005, I wrote to David, reminding him of our proposal to restructure the 33-member PPL Board to include a voting representative of the mayor, a voting representative of the governor, and four "public Trustees (who would be chosen by the mayor in consultation with the city council), to represent the users of the libraries in the different areas of the city. We also thought at that time that the Chief of Library Services for the State of RI or his/her designee, the chairperson of the Board of Education or his/her designee, and a reference librarian from one of the state's colleges or universities should be Trustees. The rest of the Board (73%) would be elected by PPL in their usual manner. "One thing I know for sure," I wrote, "is that having open meetings alone will not ensure that we do not continue to have a library that ignores the views and needs of the citizenry; we must have real representation on the Board. And presently, the PPL, although bitching and again threatening library hour cutbacks, seems to think it is a given that they will have $3,000,000 automatically."[3]

By November 2005, a clear majority of the city council supported our demands for public representatives appointed by the city on the PPL board. At a City Finance committee meeting attended by the Library director and members of PPL's board as well as by members of the public, the Finance committee suggested that 1/3 of the Board, a number that matched the proportion of the budget that was paid

3   Letter to Mayor David Cicilline from Linda J. Kushner, May 9, 2005, in author's possession.

with Providence taxpayer dollars, should be public appointees, Upon hearing this, the Board's vice chairman Howard Walker told the Council's Finance Committee that the Library would reject the City's $3,000,000 subsidy if it meant having public representation.[1] Howard also suggested that any action by the Council was premature because the library had begun its strategic planning and had recently agreed to explore the library's future with city officials.

The council, at this time, was ahead of the mayor in recognizing the intransigence of the PPL board. Mayor Cicilline, nurturing the hope that PPL would provide full services to the branches as well as maintain Central, took a cautious approach to dealing with the Library. However, the mayor was shocked by Walker's statement that the PPL would forgo public money rather than have public participation on its Board. In an interview in 2015, the mayor, looking back, said it was Walker's representation to the City Council that PPL would rather give up $3,000,000 of public funding than have public members added to the Board that made him begin to realize that PPL was truly not interested in running a public library that served the community.[2]

Really Implementing the Open Meetings Law

PPL HAD A HARD TIME COMING TO GRIPS WITH THE FACT THAT THE open meetings law truly opened decision-making at PPL to the public. At the November board meeting, I tried to use my two minutes of public comment to inform them of how extensive the mandate was. But my time ran out before I could cover the salient points. So, I

---

1 Richard C. Dujardin, "Library trustees will resist council role," *Providence Journal* (November 4, 2005).

2 Interview with David Cicilline by Ellen Schwartz, July 9, 2015. Story-Corps collection at Rochambeau Library.

wrote a three-page letter to Mary Olenn, the Chairman of the Board of Trustees, explaining what was required.[3]

The law not only covers board meetings and finance committee meetings, I informed her, but all meetings "to discuss and/or act upon over which the public body [now included PPL] has supervision, control...." Quite frankly, I myself was surprised at the breadth of the disclosure that the law demanded. When I suggested to my legislative friends that they amend RIGL 42-45, the open meetings law, by adding libraries that received a majority of their operational budget from public funds to the organizations covered, I had no idea of the extent of the law's reach. But now that it had been enacted, I certainly was going to apply every bit of it to PPL.

PPL, in violation of the law, had only posted its Board meetings and the meetings of its finance and pension committees. It had failed to post any meetings of its Executive Committee where motions were hatched that subsequently were passed pro forma by a compliant Board. It also had not posted the meetings of the Strategic Planning Commission, a new organ created by PPL ostensibly to examine a wide range of possible future actions by the Library, but ultimately to confirm the Library's intention to lop off most of its branches.

In my letter to Chairman Olenn, I referenced Howard Walker's amazing statement to the city council finance committee, which had been reported in the ProJo. "It is difficult," I wrote, "for me to believe that Mr Walker could have made such a representation to the City Council without at least the Executive Committee having met and discussed the issue and authorized Mr Walker to speak for them." No Executive Committee meetings had been posted authorizing Mr. Walker's statement.

I also warned that PPL could not avoid the open meetings law requirements by conducting its business through telephone

---

3 Letter from Linda J.Kushner to Mary B.Olenn, November 30, 2005.

conversations. RIGL 42-45-5(b) states: "No meeting of members of a public body or use of electronic communication, including telephonic communication and telephone conferencing, shall be used to circumvent the spirit or requirements of this chapter." Open meant open!

There was an amazing dearth of financial information in the reports presented at PPL meetings. At the Oct. 6th PPL finance committee, a lengthy and apparently detailed document was presented to the committee, which approved "the draft financials as presented." However, no draft report was attached to the minutes that were supplied to the public. I informed Mrs Olenn that this, too, had to be made public. The law states that "... any documents submitted at a public meeting of a public body shall be deemed public." Actually, the open records law was not that hard to understand if one wanted to. But PPL remained determined to operate in secret, notwithstanding its receipt of public funds and the passage of the law.

2006 and the Closing of the Washington Park Branch

2006 BEGAN WITH GREAT HOPE THAT THE CITY WOULD FORCE changes at the Library. The City Council took a first step toward forcing PPL to give the public more representation on the Board of Trustees. On January 23rd, the finance committee approved an ordinance that made having eight city-appointed trustees on the Board a condition of the city continuing to fund PPL. Under the ordinance, the mayor and the council would each have four appointments to the Board. The appointees were to be chosen equally from the city's four library zones: East side/Smith Hill (including the Rochambeau, Fox Point, and Smith Hill branches); the Northwest (including the Olneyville, Mount Pleasant, and Wanskuck branches); the Southside (including the Knight Memorial, South Providence, and Washington Park branches); and Central (including the Central Library and the Downtown branch). The council's concrete step toward reigning in the autocratic administration of the city's libraries may have been stimulated by PPL's sudden closing of the Washington Park branch.

The closing of Washington Park came out of the blue. It was a Friday afternoon, January 10, 2006. Ellen Schwartz, an accountant, was at the Washington Park branch as a volunteer after-school homework tutor. Ellen told us that suddenly, someone came in and said, "There is a leak in the roof. This place isn't safe, and we can't afford to keep it open." All of a sudden, the branch was closed. It was closed not just for repairs but was permanently shuttered. There were over forty kids in the library at the time of the closure, and now they and the rest of the Washington Park community were without a library. At the insistence of Councilman Aponte, PPL, a few months later, did rent space in a closed Benny's appliance store up the street to hold an after-school program from two to six on weekdays. But it was a sorry excuse for a library branch! It had two shelves of children's books. Adults were not allowed into the space to use the four computers or to pick up reserved books. And it, too, leaked.

Bob Kerr, the columnist for the Providence Journal, visited the Bennys. "It doesn't have that library feel. It doesn't have the worked-in smells of old paper and paste and polished wood. It has the feel of a place where people used to buy auto parts and lawn chairs. It's makeshift to the extreme. It's a patronizing crumb tossed to the neighborhood.... As many as 90 kids used to go to the Washington Park library in the afternoon. Down at what is derisively called the 'Benny's Library,' attendance barely hits double figures.[1]

The closing of Washington Park enraged Ellen. At first, she did

---

1   Bob Kerr, "A failure in one part of the city," Providence Journal (August 23, 2006

what she usually did. Using her knowledge as an accountant, she looked up the tax filings of PPL and found that at the time they shuttered Washington Park, PPL had more than $41,000,000 in their savings and endowment. This further enraged Ellen. She went to the City Finance committee hearing, armed with a petition signed by sixty-five neighborhood children protesting the closure. She testified in no uncertain terms that PPL had plenty of money to fix the Washington Park branch.

But then Ellen did what she had never done. She joined a group, the Library Reform Group. Ellen describes herself as a person who likes to stay in her house, prepare tax returns and other financial papers for her clients, and then relax with a good book. She does not have the patience, she explained, to go to meetings, work with groups, and schmooze with politicians. But that was the old Ellen—before the Washington Park closure!

Ellen was a godsend to the Library Reform Group. A CPA with extensive experience working with nonprofits, numbers did not frighten her. She relished analyzing budgets and tax returns. She relished the opportunity to dig into the financial records of PPL. The only trouble was that up to now, PPL's status as a private corporation had shielded most of its financial records from public scrutiny.

The sudden closing of the Washington Park branch raised the specter that PPL was deliberately allowing branch buildings to fall into disrepair in order to justify the closing of those branches. The leaks at Washington Park had been apparent since at least 2005.[1] The minutes of the October 2005 Annual Meeting meeting of PPL noted that the roof of Washington Park had badly deteriorated and should be replaced. The preliminary estimate of the cost of replacement was

---

1 Neighborhood residents told Ellen that they had offered to donate their labor to fix the leaks in 2005 before it turned into a major renovation job. Residents said that the cost of materials for the job would have been $20,000. But PPL turned them down.

$80,000. The minutes also noted that the Olneyville and Fox Point branches were known to have substantial mold problems as well as water problems. The roof at Smith Hill needed to be replaced. The failure of PPL to address physical problems at the branches before they necessitated closure was inexcusable, considering that PPL's "endowment" exceeded $36 million and that at least $20 million of it was not truly endowment but were funds that the Board had parked in the "endowment account." As such, this money was available and could have been used to protect and maintain the value of its buildings.

The legislation to increase public representation on the PPL board, introduced in the City Council at the beginning of the year, faced an uphill battle on two fronts. The Library thought such a motion was premature, if not unnecessary, and the mayor, who at that time still nurtured the dream of PPL continuing to provide full library services to the city, was hesitant to antagonize it.

PPL wanted to address governance issues at the Library through the Strategic Planning Commission it had created to analyze the future of the Library. PPL's director, Dale Thompson, told the Council, "While the oversight of public funds for Library services is already provided in the quarterly reports to the City Council, the Providence Public Library recognizes the interest of some city councilors for more oversight of public funds appropriate for Library services. We agree to work toward a new arrangement with the City of Providence and have proposed it [the Council] to be part of the joint strategic planning process in which the Library and the City are currently engaged."[2]

Less than a month after its introduction, the Council's ambitious library restructuring proposal came to an ignominious pause. The Council tabled its own legislation. Library Reform group members thought that the Council had paused its formal demands for public representation on the Board because the PPL Board was ready to

---

2   Cathleen F. Crowley, "Councilors move to expand city influence over Library,"*Providence Journal* (January 24, 2006).

engage in discussion with the City and reach a compromise position. We went to the next PPL board meeting on February 6th, expecting some action. Instead, the Board passed, without discussion, a resolution stating that they would be willing to discuss the issue with the mayor and city council at some unspecific time. Pressed by a reporter, Mary Olenn, Board Chair, said that they had no intention of taking a position on the makeup of the Board until they have completed work on the strategic plan, which she did not expect to be finished until May.

Considering that the city's fiscal year starts July 1st, it was fairly clear that PPL had no intention of addressing the issue of Board structure before the City would have to vote in June on a budget for Fiscal 07. To add insult to injury, the Board ignored Councilman Luis A. Aponte and Councilman David Segal, who had come to the February 6th PPL meeting in expectation of hearing the Board discuss the Council's proposed plan. When the board did not address the issue, the two councilmen left in disgust.

Meanwhile, PPL was once again threatening to cut library services in the city if there was not a substantial increase of funding for PPL in fiscal 07. In March, they testified to the city council's finance committee that the Library expected a deficit in its budget of $700,000 for the next fiscal year as well as a possible shortfall in the budget for privately funded programs and capital costs.[1] The likelihood of mutual resolution on the governance and funding of PPL looked grim.

In April, Library Reform Group members rallied at City Hall as the Council restarted its work on the ordinance to place eight City-appointed members on the PPL board. On April 7th, the ordinance had its first passage through the City Council. But there was still a long way to go. The Providence City Council is a unicameral body. Legislation must pass twice through the Council before it can be signed into law by the mayor.

---

1 Karen A. Davis, "Officials sat deficit looms over library," *Providence Journal* (March 2, 2006).

On April 11th, five days after the first passage of the ordinance, the executive committee of PPL proposed closing six branches: Fox Point, Smith Hill, Olneyville, Knight Memorial, Wanskuck, and Washington Park (already shut down) if the city did not increase their funding to $3.7 million.[2] They explained that these library closures and attendant staff cuts would provide $900,000 in savings.

The proposed ordinance and the actions of PPL prompted a rash of letters and op-eds. The Providence Journal, at this time still carrying water for PPL, declared, "Members of the Providence City Council, seeking a campaign issue and perhaps a place for patronage, have been harassing the Providence Public Library." They went on to suggest that "PPL should seriously consider giving the City of Providence any or all of its branches while keeping its flagship facility on Empire Street."[3]

The next day, in an opinion piece published in the ProJo, Council President John Lombardi observed: "In 2004, the library administration stated that one reason for the layoff and reduced hours [downtown] was that these measures would allow all 10 (sic) neighborhood branches to remain open. Yet, only two years later, Providence is facing the possibility of only four of these branches remaining open and more layoffs on the way."[4] Replying to cries of alarm by PPL and the ProJo, he wrote: "What the City Council is proposing is not revolutionary and would have only a modest impact on the library's governing structure. The council is not seeking a fundamental change in the operations of the library. Nor does the council wish to take over the branches or become involved in day-to-day oversight."

The Library Reform Group signed in the following day with an

---

2   Sheila Lennon, "Library Lookup updated, new instructions for IE users," *Providence Journal* (April 12, 2006).

3   Editorial, "Spin off library branches,"Providence Journal, (April 17, 2006).

4   Councilman John Lombardi, Editorial "Library branch closings cause for alarm,"*Providence Journal* P (April 18, 2006).

opinion piece authored by Deborah Schimberg, the Chair of Save our Branches, and Patricia Raub, the Chair of the Library Reform Group. "The recent proposal of the Library's Finance committee to close six branches, primarily those servicing the least affluent city neighborhoods, and the rush by library leaders to divest themselves of the responsibility of running the branch libraries constitute a reaction to the threat of a greater public participation in library governance that is simplistic, premature and harmful to the community," they wrote. "There are many other ways to deal with the budget shortfall without punishing the community, including more belt-tightening on the purchase of library resources, a reduction of the salaries of the top library administrators, a decision by the board to use some of the $2 million in unrestricted funds to deal with a part of the problems, or agreement to share the costs of covering the deficit equally among the city, the state, and the library.... The Providence community is not asking to control the libraries, just to have a seat at the table where the decisions affecting Library users throughout the city are made."[1]

More letters attacking the Library's proposal and decrying the ProJo's castigation of the City Council piled in during the following week. The state's General Assembly passed a resolution in support of public members being appointed to the PPL board.

Although we were being stymied once again in our effort to change the structure of PPL's Board, another development took me by surprise. It appears that you can't scream for more than a year without someone noticing you. And that was what happened to the Library Reform Group. News articles now began their reports about the library situation with statements about us. The lead sentence in the ProJo on Feb. 7th started with "To the consternation of members of a library-reform group..." Then, one day, while reading PPL's minutes, I came across a term that was unfamiliar "LRG." What is this LRG

---

1   Deborah Schimberg and Patricia Raub, "Commentary -Save the PPL branches," *Providence Journal* (April 19, 2006).

they are writing about, I mused. Then I realized it was us! PPL and the public recognized the Library Reform Group was not a flash in the pan. We had become a permanent irksome factor in library politics.

Although Dale Thompson always maintained an icy pleasantness, our monthly appearance at the PPL board meetings really annoyed some board members. One time, after a meeting, Mary Olenn, the Chair of the Board, came up to me as I was packing up my papers. "You think you can run the Library better than we do," she said to me. "No," I replied, "we just want you to do a better job of running it." Truly, we had not thought of replacing the Library; we just wanted to reform it.

The Strategic Planning Commission

MEANWHILE, WHAT OF THE STRATEGIC PLANNING COMMISSION, THE Library's silver bullet to solve its problem? The commission was created in November 2005. Sam Frank of Synthesis Partnership had been hired as the consultant. He had announced that a plan would be fully developed and approved by March 2006.

The participants from PPL included Dale Thompson, four PPL Board members, and a librarian from the Central Library. Joe Fernandez, the mayor's representative on the Board, and Mark McKenney, the Chair of the Library Board of Rhode Island (who shortly would join the PPL Board as the governor's representative) were participants. Gary Bliss, the city's director of policy and legislative affairs, represented the city. There were three public appointees: Hilary Salmons of the Education Partnership; Joyce Butler, the director of Ready to Learn (both agencies supplied educational services to the Library); and Deborah Wyatt, the director of the West End Neighborhood Center. Although the commission did have some representatives who were not part of PPL, it did not have any community members who had studied the management of PPL and were critical of it. The commission was staffed by PPL administrators, including Maureen

Sheridan, PPL's Director of Institutional Advancement, who at times ran roughshod over known critics of the library.

From the beginning, the Commission, although formed to explore many plans for the Library's future development, appeared to be a put-up job to justify PPL's actions to reduce library services in the city of Providence. The consultants, costing $70,000, prepared elaborate sociological and statistical studies, but their conclusions appeared to have been foreordained—to reduce the Providence Public Library system to the Central Library and four branches: the three large branches (Rochambeau, Mt Pleasant, and Knight Memorial) and the South Providence branch which had just been completely renovated.

PPL had promised that the Commission, which began meeting in November 2005, would produce a model for the best, most sustainable structure for PPL by the spring of 2006. But, by March, they were nowhere near the end. In an effort to placate an enraged city council, PPL offered to increase the number of community representatives on the Commission from three to six, with the Council appointing the new members. The council seized the opportunity to put three members of the Library Reform Group—Elaine Heebner, Rochelle Lee, and myself—on the Commission.

Our entry onto the Commission was a bit dramatic. Time was of the essence, we naively thought, if our presence was to make any difference in the deliberations of the Commission. Councilman David Segal had told us we had been appointed, but we weren't sure the appointment had gone through the necessary procedural hoops to allow us to take our places on the commission. The next meeting of the Commission was March 9th. Uncertain of our status, the three of us went to the meeting and sat in the area reserved for observers. Then the meeting started. Suddenly, I received a phone call from Patricia Raub who was at City Hall. Yes, the appointment had been officially registered, and we were Commission members. With that confirmation, we got up from our observers' seats and moved to the table where the other commissioners sat.

We had hoped to influence the deliberations. But though we now had a seat at the table, the Commission continued to march to the tune of PPL. On March 28th, the Commission held an all-day retreat at which we had the opportunity to present our position to the Commission. We made seven recommendations:

1. That the original nine library branches be maintained and remain open to the public for a substantial number of hours per week based on the community needs.
2. That the PPL board prudently explore using a portion of the endowment that has not been restricted by the donors to repair PPL buildings that had been allowed to deteriorate to the extent that they threaten the continued branch operation.
3. That the collections and services at the downtown library be reunified as a single Central Library entity and that the "Empire Street Branch" designation be discontinued.
4. That the library book budget be increased.
5. That the PPL abandon its policy of supporting the branches only to the extent they were funded by the city.
6. That the salaries of administrators who received more than $100,000 be reduced by 10% and that they forgo a raise in 2006 (money saved to go to branch operating funds)
7. That one month before any action seriously curtailing services at a branch, the public and City Council be notified of the proposed action, given all relevant financial information; and that there be a public hearing at the Library before any action is taken.

Of course, this was a bit like spitting into the wind. The writing was already on the wall. At a commission meeting on March 23, Sam Frank had floated a proposal for eliminating all but two existing branches. The next day, Lisa Churchville, the vice-chairman of PPL's Board, proposed a plan that only retained one branch! Then, at a May

5th retreat of the Commission, Frank revealed the "foreordained" plan of "four premier libraries throughout the city."

Finally, on June 30th, after more meetings and more day long retreats, the Commission issued its 104-page report. Beautifully bound and stuffed with charts and strategic-planning team documents, the report did not really represent much of a change from the PPL position previewed at the PPL Executive Committee meeting in April 2006, where it recommended closing six branches.[1] The report recommended the path PPL had already embraced, that the branches be reduced to three or four larger branches serving different sections of the city, and that these branches be open for longer hours. It suggested that the city and Library "find a way to keep all branches open during a limited, clearly defined interim period while any changes in library services delivery are agreed to through face-to-face discussion."[2] Beyond that, the report seemed to suggest that PPL look for sites to use as joint-use sites and or co-locations where some library services, such as public computers, could be located. Then it recommended the no-brainer admonition: "The only way for these issues to be resolved successfully and without disruption in library services in the city is for representatives of the City and the PPL board to sit down with a willingness to look at compromise solutions—not to insist on approaches that are out of the question to the other side—and negotiate a written agreement."

Even though we had known from the get-go that the Strategic Planning Commission was only an expensive boondoggle designed to give PPL cover while it proceeded with its plans to eliminate branches, we three Library Reform Representatives soldiered on. We presented an alternative report listing the factors that undermined

---

1 Cathleen F. Crowley, "Providence Library proposes closing 6 branches,"*Providence Journal* (April 12, 2006).
2 Synthesis Partnership and Dubberly Garcia Associates, Inc, "Providence Public Library Strategic Plan" June 30, 2006.

the accuracy and usefulness of the Commission's report. Of course, we again stressed that PPL should maintain all nine neighborhood branches and that PPL needed public input on its Board of Trustees if it were to regain public trust.

Meanwhile, the City Council was coming face to face with the second impediment to its enactment of the ordinance that would add eight publicly appointed people to the board of PPL. Mayor Cicilline was against it. As Cicilline later shared in an interview in 2015,[3] he had hated the idea of breaking up PPL, an institution that, for better or worse, had provided library services to the city for 135 years. Surely, he thought, there had to be a way to work out a compromise with the Library and get its agreement to have a few more publicly appointed people on its Board.

But PPL, violently opposed to the proposed ordinance, unveiled its biggest threat: the city itself would have to take over the job of providing library services to its residents. This was a non-starter, and PPL knew it. The city, already strapped for cash, could hardly afford to create its own Department of library services.

The Steinberg Report

On April 22, 2006, as the tension between the Council and PPL reached the boiling point, the mayor appointed Neil D. Steinberg, a former banker who was vice president of development at Brown University, to conduct an independent review of PPL's financial resources and how it allocated its money. The review would also study the costs of the branches and who used them. The mayor prevailed on the Council to postpone its second passage of the ordinance until Steinberg had clarified the Library's financial situation. PPL agreed

3 Interview with David Cicilline by Ellen Schwartz, July 9, 2015. Story-Corps collection at Rochambeau Library.

to allow Steinberg to review their records and promised to postpone their vote on their 2007 budget, which included layoffs and branch closings.

The mayor rejoiced with this breathing space. "The branches are the heart and soul of our library system," he said to the ProJo. "My own goal is to ensure that we protect our library and the branch system. Library branches are for so many of our kids and families their only access to computers, books, and a host of after-school programs."[1] Cicilline said he'd consider reconfiguring the branches, such as co-locating a branch in a new school building. Also, he did not rule out giving PPL more money if the Steinberg report supported it.

Pause or not, the rallies and protests continued. On May 8th, more than 150 people marched up Washington Street to demonstrate at the Central Library. "The protest attracted people from every branch and from every demographic of the city," the *Providence Journal* reported.[2] After rallying in front of the building, the demonstrators entered the library and marched silently through the newly created Empire Street branch and the children's room on the first floor. "Tensions are rising over a growing deficit and the possibility that the branches in some neighborhoods could close," a lead sentence in the *ProJo* announced in a long article published on May 14th.[3]

On May 20th, an after-school rally outside of the Knight Memorial branch organized by middle school children to protest PPL's plan to shutter six branches attracted a large group of students, parents, and, of course, library reformers. The focus of the rally was the students'

---

1 Cathleen F. Crowley, "Providence library faces a crossroads," *Providence Journal* (May 14, 2006).

2 Cathleen F. Crowley, "No libraries, no future – protesters won't go with plan to shelve branches," *Providence Journal* (May 9, 2006).

3 Cathleen F. Crowley, "Providence library faces a crossroads," *Providence Journal* (May 14, 2006).

fear of losing the after-school programs at Knight and other branches if the Library shut the six branches. On June 16th, at a rally in front of Smith Hill Library, ten city groups announced that they had formed a coalition in support of library reform. The coalition was composed of the Smith Hill Friends, Mount Pleasant Friends, the newly formed Wanskuck Friends, Library Reform Group, Save our Branches, Smith Hill Community Development Association, Providence Community Health Centers, and the Institute for the Study and Practice of Nonviolence. The creation of this coalition marked the first time institutions not primarily concerned with libraries formally joined the fight to reform the PPL.[4] A state legislator announced at the rally that he would be introducing legislation in the General Assembly to deal with the problem. All this was too much for the editorial board of the ProJo. On June 25th, it opined: "Providence politicians and some other citizens are upset about staff and service cutbacks at the Providence Public Library, a private nonprofit institution- not a public agency, as many people think."[5]

Meanwhile, Neil Steinberg was conducting his review of the Providence Public Library. One person who was very excited about Steinberg reviewing the heretofore rarely examined financial records of PPL was Ellen Schwartz. Ellen had spent hours pouring over all the PPL records she could get her hands on, and she had concluded that PPL's claim that the entirety of its $36 million was endowment and could not be touched was not true. Ellen pointed out that there was a difference between truly endowed funds (those which the donors had designated as endowment) and funds that the PPL Board had decided *sua sponte* to record as endowment. By Ellen's account, $20,000,000 of what PPL called its endowment were simply funds that PPL had parked in the "endowment account," and as such, these funds could

---

4 Cathleen F. Crowley, "Bill would hike library's public representation," *Providence Journal* (June 27, 2006).

5 Editorial, *Providence Journal* (June 25, 2006).

be used by the Library should it choose to address current problems such as temporary deficits and needed building repairs.

Ellen questioned the wisdom of PPL's refusal to use any of its funds to prevent closings. She argued that if the library had used more of its private funds for upkeep, the buildings would not be in such disrepair. "I am a great believer in fiscal responsibility. I think saving money for the future is a great idea. But there are times when you have to dig into your savings account—if your kids are sick or your roof is leaking or you're thinking of closing 2/3 of your branches."[1]

Ellen also contested how PPL allocated the costs of running the separate branches. She was delighted to learn that Steinberg's review would include a review of how PPL calculated the costs of running the branches.

On June 30th, Neil Steinberg presented his report to the mayor.[2] The Steinberg report, unlike the Strategic Planning Report, was short, direct, and readable. After reviewing the accounts, Steinberg found that PPL's likely operating deficit in FY 07 would be $500,000, not $700,000, as PPL had projected. He solomonically suggested that to close this deficit, the city and PPL split the cost: that the city increase its allocation by up to $250,000 and PPL commit to using up to $250,000 of its investment assets for operating expenditures if needed. The support would be pro-rata and provided at the time the FY 07 deficit was actually realized.

He recommended that the city not require public representation on the PPL Board during FY 07. Instead, he suggested that some public members be part of a ten-person group made up of mayoral and City Council representatives and some "new more politically savvy and neutral representatives from the Board" (not current PPL

---

1 Ellen Schwartz, "Is the library really broke?" *RI Policy Reporter*, (May 22, 2006).

2 "Providence Public Library Review," submitted to Mayor David N. Cicilline June 30, 2006, by Neil D. Steinberg

leadership) who would develop a three-to-five-year plan for delivery of Library services by March 31, 2007. Steinberg came down very hard on PPL leadership. "I believe," he wrote, "that the deteriorating relationship between PPL leadership, the city, and various community advocacy groups has been negatively impacted by the approach taken by the PPL leadership. As the attempt to establish a long-term solution continues, it is evident the change in the PPL leadership and board leadership should be considered."[3] He also found the fundraising efforts of the PPL wanting, although he noted that it is harder to raise funds from the public when you are cutting services.

Steinberg questioned PPL's claim that all $35,000,000 of its investments were truly restricted endowed funds, with the requirement that the principal not be spent. Like Ellen, he found that only $15,000,000 of it was actually a donor-designated endowment that could not be spent. The remaining $20,000,000, while labeled restricted funds by the Board, could, in truth, be made available for expenditures. He suggested that "consideration should be given to utilizing a prudent portion of the investment balance for a one-time expenditure to repair critical facilities." [4]

Steinberg also criticized PPL's recent practice of designating responsibility for the branches solely to the City, in effect limiting the funds available for the support of the branches to money allocated by the City, as unreasonable. He dismissed PPL's idea of a separate corporate board for managing the city funds that PPL would earmark for the branches. "It is not reasonable to consider separation of the responsibility for branch operations from the central library services since investment income is now used to support the entire combined operation."[5]

---

3   "Providence Public Library Review" by Neil D. Steinberg, p. 9.

4   "Providence Public Library Review" by Neil D. Steinberg, p. 11.

5   "Providence Public Library Review" by Neil D. Steinberg, p. 12.

Steinberg offered the view that leadership and communication, more than the structure, were the issues. He advised that a change in structure only be undertaken after a serious, long-range study of the problem.

The Response to the Steinberg Report

NOTWITHSTANDING THE ADVICE IN THE STEINBERG REPORT, PPL immediately embarked on another step to mislead the public. At their board meeting on July 10th, the Board voted unilaterally to create a new corporation to oversee taxpayer money spent on the branches.[1] This occurred while Neil Steinberg himself sat silently in the audience, waiting to formally present his report to the board. More than forty of us had come to hear his report. But in a colossal misinterpretation of the open meetings law, Board Chairwoman Mary Olenn ruled that Steinberg could not speak because the report was not on the agenda. Of course, this need not have stopped the Board from allowing him to present his report. The open meetings law allows a board to amend and add an issue to its agenda by a majority vote. But blessed with ignorance and arrogance, the Board denied him a chance to present the report. Finally, at the public comment time at the end of the meeting, Steinberg was given his two minutes to speak. He was able to present the salient points, but of course, since it was "public comment," there was no interchange or questioning of Steinberg by the Board members. The forty of us who had come to the Board meeting specifically to hear Steinberg speak were shocked at this appalling lack of respect by the Board for the expert who had been appointed by the mayor to study the problem.

It looked like, even after the Steinberg report, there was a real

---

1   Cathleen F. Crowley, "Separate board proposed for branch libraries," Providence Journal (June 30, 2006).

standoff. The mayor was not happy. As reported in the *ProJo* the following day, "he stopped short of calling for Library officials to step down but said trust must be restored in the library leadership."[2] The City Council went so far as to approve an FY 07 budget that withheld the library's $3 million allocation pending progress in city/library relations. The city also did not transfer its fourth-quarter payment to the library that would have covered expenses from April through June 2006

The Library Reform Group was outraged. "We've felt at every turn that the [PPL] administration has not shown good judgment, and perhaps we've reached the dead end with this administration and the board leadership," said Patricia Raub, chairwoman of the reform group. "Until change happens at the top, we aren't going to restore confidence in the Library, no matter how many reports we have."[3]

During the week, op-eds poured into the ProJo. Finally, on July 21st, the City and PPL adopted Neil Steinberg's formula; each side ponied up $250,000 to prevent the closure of the branches, and a budget for FY 07 was passed.

The Municipal Working Group

BUT PLANS FOR THE FUTURE DID NOT GIVE US REFORMERS MUCH HOPE. The council announced, in line with the recommendation of the Steinberg Report, that there would be a nine-person committee, "the Municipal Working Group," to develop a contract between the City and PPL for library services. It would have three city representatives, three Library representatives, and three independent members. The city council indicated they were thinking of naming Neil Steinberg, Mark

2 Cathleen F. Crowley, "City, library look to move forward," *Providence Journal* (July 12, 2006).
3 Cathleen F Crowley, "City, library look to move forward," Providence Journal (July 12, 2006).

McKenney (the governor's appointee on the Library board of trustees), and Sam Frank (the consultant who generated the Strategic Planning Commission Report). At the mention of Frank's name, as reported in the *Providence Journal*, Library advocates in the audience gasped. "Mr. Frank is a very skilled person, but he really is not a person to be on this board," I testified before the city council. "We already have $70,000 worth of Mr. Frank that actually undermined the community input."[1]
I ARGUED INSTEAD FOR A LIBRARY PATRON TO SERVE ON THE GROUP."

But the walls of officialdom were shutting us out. While City Council members supported having the public in the group, John Simmons, the mayor's director of administration, said that "a member of the public on the working group might prevent the candid discussions necessary during negotiation."[2]

There was a fundamental difference between how we viewed the function of the Municipal Working Group and how PPL and the mayor's office each viewed it. PPL believed the Library was a private corporation and that it alone, should make all decisions regarding the running of the Library. It agreed that some stakeholders should be consulted with respect to particular decisions, but it limited stakeholders only to the city and state, who funded part of the Library's operations. The mayor's office, although aware of and sympathetic to the public's need for community representation, regarded the commission as the forum for the negotiation of a contract between the city and the Library for library services. The city believed it acted in the public's interest. Library advocates, however, thought library users who funded part of the Library's operation through their taxes were central stakeholders who themselves should have separate representation in the group that would plan the Library's future.

---

1 Cathleen F Crowley, "Council accepts library review recommendations" *Providence Journal* (July 21, 2006).

2 Cathleen F Crowley, "Council accepts library review recommendation." *Providence Journal* (July 21, 2006).

In August, the mayor appointed Neil Steinberg, Mark McKinney, and Sam Frank as the three public representatives. Reform advocates were truly left in the cold. Stung by our exclusion from the Municipal Working Group that was to design the contract between the city and PPL for library services, we library advocates hurriedly met that weekend and decided that we would form a separate coalition to conduct a parallel analysis of the Library's operation and its future.

The Library Advocates Coalition

ON AUGUST 16TH, PATRICIA RAUB ANNOUNCED THE CREATION OF A nine-person Library Advocates Coalition, a group made up of librarians and patrons who lived in Providence, that would augment the conversation taking place between the city and PPL. "Some of us are librarians, all of us are patrons of the library, and we have been advocates of the library for two years. I think we offered the missing public perspective."[3] The coalition, she announced, would hold public forums on the issues of the affordability of maintaining nine neighborhood branches, the feasibility of maintaining a strong central library and statewide services, the cost of the staff and programs, a fiscal plan that would keep central library and branches intact, and the structure of the library governance.

Library Reformers mounted a major campaign to "Put the PUBLIC into the Providence Public Library." Each of us mined our contacts to bring people to rallies and gain widespread public support. We sent letters to labor unions, politicians, community organizers, social agencies, church groups, and advocates of any kind to get them involved in our campaign to keep the nine branches open and to have public representation on the PPL board. We set

---

3   Catherine F Crowley, "Library advocates form new coalition," *Providence Journal* (August 16, 2006).

up meetings at each of the branches to explain to the community what was really happening. And we made sure that when PPL itself held a rare meeting at a branch, we were there to raise questions. We printed thousands of blue Library Reform Group bookmarks showing a young boy reading and articulating our primary goal, "Put the Public in Providence Public Library." Although the bookmark was handed out relentlessly at every public gathering, Patricia and I still have some. It is my favorite bookmark.

Attempts to Reopen Washington Park

THE MOST MEMORABLE AND FUN EVENT OF 2006 WAS A READ-IN organized by Ellen Schwartz in the little park next to the shuttered Washington Park branch. There, on a beautiful October afternoon, more than one hundred people gathered to listen to children's stories read by readers ranging from professional actors from Trinity Repertory Theater and the Black Story Tellers to more amateur readers like city councilors and library reformers. Each of us read a well-loved children's story to the children and adults gathered there. It was wonderful to sit in the warm sun and watch the listening children laugh with glee as we read our favorites. When it was my turn, I read *The Little Train That Could*, a childhood favorite of mine, which seemed to me to sum up the whole situation. Councilman Luna, a labor organizer, read the book *Click Clack Moo*, a funny story about farm animals revolting and organizing a labor union. But a ten-year-old girl who had just moved to the Washington Park neighborhood confided indignantly to Ellen Schwartz, "Where we lived, we had a real library, not just a story hour." Ellen felt the child's anger.[1]

"Everybody needs the library...not just children," Ellen told the crowd. Listening to this was Allen Shawn Feinstein, a well-known

---

1 Personal conversation with Ellen Schwartz November 12, 2023.

"Ellen Schwartz at the Washington Park Read-Out," Providence Journal
October 2006, Kris Craig, photographer.

philanthropist who had grown up in Washington Park and used that branch as a child. Feinstein offered a $100,000 challenge to PPL and the city to help renovate the building. This offer was brushed aside by PPL under the guise of needing a comprehensive plan to be in place for the future of this and all library buildings used to deliver municipal library services in the city before they could reopen Washington Park. Clearly, the Library was not interested in the opinions and even the dollars of the community.

The read-in also galvanized the resolve of neighborhood church leaders. Rev. Duane Clinker of The Open Table of Christ United Methodist Church, located a few blocks from the closed branch, was determined to have the Washington Park library reopened. Six months later, in April 2007, with Washington Park still closed, Rev. Clinker, Rev. Jeffrey Williams of The Cathedral of Life, and Sister Anne Keefe of St. Michael's, the large Catholic parish church in South

Providence, met with the mayor, asking for a date when Washington Park Library would be repaired and reopened. It had been closed for fifteen months.

Sister Anne Keefe was a force to be reckoned with. A remarkable woman, she had already created the Providence City Arts for Youth, which had its own building in the west end, and had enrolled 1200 children yearly in after-school and summer programs. She also co-founded The Institute for the Study and Practice of Non-Violence in South Providence, which was credited with having helped to sharply cut the city's murder rate. Now, she was squarely behind the library reform effort. She told me in a phone call at that time that she thought our reform campaign "was absolutely essential."

At a meeting with the church leaders in April 2007, the mayor promised to provide $400,000 in city money to repair the roof. But he put conditions on this funding: the trustees would have to keep the branch at its current site. The Church leaders met with Dale Thompson a few weeks later, but there was still no commitment by the Library to reopen the branch in its present home. Once again, the people of Washington Park faced a summer without their own library.

2007 More of Nothing

DESPITE THE ONE-YEAR AGREEMENT BETWEEN THE BOARD AND THE city based upon Steinberg's recommendations, which had allowed for a deficit budget and the same level of library service while the Municipal Working Group identified options for the future, the city and the Library continued to squabble. This time, they squabbled over the timing of the payments.

By the spring of 2007, the PPL Board was careening from one wild idea to another. In February, the ProJo revealed that Dale Thompson had been talking to real estate firms to see what the sale of the Central Library building would garner. The 115,000 square-foot central library building, built in the Italian Renaissance style at Washington and Empire Street in 1900, was on the National Register of Historic Places. It had been valued by the city at $16 million in the late 1990s. "We may be sitting on a $16 million that could be put to a different use," said Lisa Churchville, then the Chair of the PPL Board of Trustees.[1] But this evaluation, in my opinion, was pie-in-the-sky. The building had no parking. And the fact that it was on the historic register made it very unlikely that anyone would approve of tearing it down. In fact, the only offer they had received to date for it was $387,000.

Then, at the March 2007 PPL Board meeting, the Library announced that they wanted the city to increase its contribution to the libraries from $3 million annually to $5 million unless the City would establish its own oversight board to run the nine branch libraries.[2] In the latter case, the city would need to pay PPL $3.8 million. Incredibly, PPL offered no increase in services in return for the gigantic hike in funds they were asking for. Rob Taylor, a trustee, assured the listening audience that the Library had formed a transition team that could come up with contingency plans if the city and the library did not reach an agreement before the start of the fiscal year. He warned that without the increased funding, there could be layoffs of fifteen to twenty library employees. Contingency plans could include placing some of the branches "in mothballs" for the year if no agreement could be reached. It was fourteen weeks to the start of the new fiscal year, and the Mayor's Municipal Working Group had not come up with a solution. PPL was now suggesting that either the City pay PPL $5 million for running the branches or that the city take over all the branches and run them as a city department.

PPL's proposal raised alarms. Its timing ruffled the feathers of

---

1 Daniel Barbarisi, "Central Library may be put up for sale.," *Providence Journal (February* 16, 2007).

2 Daniel Barbarisi, "Library seeks one-year pact with the city for $5 million," *Providence Journal (*March 16, 2007).

"Mayor David Cicilline at Rally at Knight Memorial"
Providence Journal, *May 2006.*

the Mayor's Municipal Working Group, which was still working on developing a solution to the city//PPL problem. The two sides (the city and PPL) had agreed not to publicly say anything before the Municipal Working Group issued its report. But that agreement had obviously been broken by PPL. In April, amping up the pressure on the city, PPL issued pink slips (layoff notices) to sixty employees.

Meanwhile, library reformers were attending unending meetings. Besides the regular meetings of the Library Reform Group held at my house and the meetings of the Library Advocates Coalition, we organized and commandeered every community meeting to further our goals.

In January, the Library Advocates Coalition sponsored a forum on library governance at Rochambeau. It featured Emily Badger, director of

Blue Bookmark

the Springfield Massachusetts City Library, and David Macksam, director of the Cranston Rhode Island Library, both of whom had hands-on knowledge of library governance. Ms Badger's library had been a private library taken over by the city of Springfield. The public library run by Dave Macksam in neighboring Cranston had more branches per capita than the Providence Public Library. We thought these professionals could bring real knowledge to the question of the feasibility and desirability of financing and operating a multi-branch library system. The Library Reform Group made a point of inviting city councilors as well as individual PPL Board members to come and learn from the discussion.

By the end of February 2007, the Library Advocates Coalition, which had been meeting regularly since its creation in 2006, issued a report, covered in the *ProJo*, calling for the replacement of the library's director and other top administrators. "The public has lost confidence in the library's leadership, and change is needed to move forward."[1] With respect to funding, the Coalition recommended that the city increase its donation by fifteen percent and that the library trim its overhead by fifteen percent, particularly by chopping administrative salaries. And, of course, the report asked for five publicly appointed members to be placed on the board, three appointed by the City Council and two by the mayor.

Keeping all nine branches was a basic tenant for us reformers. The importance and uniqueness of each branch were made clear by Althea Graves as she described her own branch, Smith Hill, "as part community meeting hall, part after school haven, and part corner hangout. We are a community city. If you shut any down, there's a problem.... Where will we go? It's also a social area where you meet and greet your neighbors. I don't want to go to Rochambeau and meet and greet with strangers."[2]

In May, in an effort to pressure the city to agree to their demands, PPL took a page from the reformers and decided to take its case to the public. It scheduled eight meetings at the branches. The Library Reform Group welcomed these meetings as an opportunity to present our case and to hold PPL administrators accountable. Patricia Raub told the ProJo reporter covering the story that these meetings should be held whether the two sides had reached an agreement or not. In a letter sent to a growing army of reformers, she wrote, "These neighborhood meetings will be an important venue for us to make our voices heard and hold the Providence Public Library to account for dragging its feet...It would be worthwhile to show up at your local library's scheduled meeting and ask the PPL administrators some hard questions."[3]

---

1 Daniel Barbarisi, "Library group urges major changes, retaining branches," *Providence Journal* (February 27, 2007).

2 Personal interview with Althea Graves January 12, 2023.

3 Daniel Barbarisi, "Library taking its financial message to public forums," *Providence Journal* (May 1, 2007).

And show up, we did. Armed with flyers proclaiming that "the public is not being served as well as it could be," we intermingled with branch patrons concerned about how their branch was being treated. We used these meetings to grow our movement. And, of course, we distributed the ubiquitous blue Library Reform Group bookmarks that demanded that "The Public Be Put in the Providence Public Library!"

It seemed that the city and Library would never agree on a contract for FY 08, much less incorporate the changes we advocated. At one point during one of the innumerable meetings of the Library Reform Group at my house, Althea Graves, whose small library, Smith Hill, was always on the chopping block, leaned over to Rochelle Lee and Elaine Heebner, who were sitting near her and suggested that we give up trying to change PPL. They were just too intractable, she reminded her neighbors who themselves had long experience dealing with PPL, Elaine as a former employee, and Rochelle as a social advocate in South Providence. "We should think about creating a separate library," she suggested. Elaine and Rochelle, she remembered, seemed to agree with her.[4] But neither Patricia nor I, who were running the meeting, remember hearing the suggestion. It certainly was not taken up then. In retrospect, we were not equipped at that time to undertake such an operation.

Finally, on June 13, 2007, the City and PPL agreed to a one-year renewable contract.[5] Even though the library announced that it would be reducing hours at the branches and possibly laying off some employees, the city agreed to increase its contribution by $300,000, giving the Library a total of $3.3 million this year. The city also committed to spending $400,000 for a Washington Park branch either to renovate the old firehouse that had housed the branch before its sudden closure

---

4 Personal interview with Althea Graves January 12, 2023.

5 Daniel Barbarisi, "Mayor and library finally agree to one-year contract," *Providence Journal* (June 14, 2007).

in January 2006 or to find another building in the neighborhood to refit for as the library branch. The city's contributions to the Library would increase each subsequent year with the rise in the cost of living.

The larger governance proposals that each side had harbored were again shelved: the Library had wanted the city to take over the branches; the city had wanted more public appointees on the PPL board. Neither of these objectives was obtained. Instead, the Library agreed to the establishment of an advisory board—the Library Partnership Advisory Committee—made up of public, city, school, and library appointees that would have full access to the library's finances and would advise the board but have no authority over the trustees.

In case you are having trouble keeping track of all these committees, let me review them for you.

1. First, there was the "Strategic Planning Commission," created by PPL in 2005 to bolster its plan of eliminating five branches. True to its mission, this boondoggle committee of sixteen people (despite the opposition of its three library reformer members) issued in 2006, at the cost of $70,000, a report calling for the elimination of five branches.

2. Then, the "Municipal Working Group" was formed in 2007 as a result of a recommendation in the Steinberg Report to issue within a year a contract for FY 08 between the city and PPL. It was composed of nine members, none of whom were reformers or even library patrons.

3. In response to being locked out of the deliberations on the contract, we reformers created an alternative committee, the "Library Advocates Coalition," made up of librarians and patrons, to give the public perspective on the problem.

4. And now nestled in the FY 08 contract was a fourth committee, the" Library Partnership Advisory Committee."

I was irate at the proposed contract and wrote so in no uncertain terms in an Op-Ed published in the *ProJo* on June 21, 2007. The funny thing was that I was not in the United States at this time. Instead, I was in Antarctica on a cruise with my husband, exploring the habitat of penguins. But thanks to the internet, I was fully informed of what was happening at home. And it was too much for me.

I carefully made my way up to the little room on the top deck of the ship, where an old public computer was attached to a small table. It was a good thing that it was attached because the ship was rocking violently. I had trouble keeping the chair, which unfortunately had wheels, from rolling away from the table. Hanging onto a post next to the table with my left hand, I carefully pecked out an email to Bob Whitcomb, the *ProJo* Op-Ed page editor. "You can take a girl out of Providence," I typed, "but you can't take the Providence library out of her." I then explained to him that I was writing from the rocking deck of a boat in Antarctica, and I begged him to print the Op-Ed I was sending. Perhaps because he was tickled by the international source of my request, he published it.

"Having studied the Providence Public Library for the last three years," I wrote, "I am exasperated but not surprised by the bargain struck between the city administration and the PPL that now has Providence taxpayers paying an additional $300,000 or more to the PPL for fewer hours of service at the branches. Equally disturbing is that the contract does not address management decisions at PPL that have contributed to the problem.... Nothing in the agreement ties the city's increase in support to an equal increase of support from the PPL. (PPL's contribution to the library has actually decreased in recent years.)...Nothing in the agreement ties the city's support to PPL's performance in raising donations to the library.... It is apparent that this year's heralded meeting between the city and the PPL has done nothing to alter the arrogant, patriarchal attitude of the PPL board, which, notwithstanding its mismanagement of the library for the last three years, continues to believe that its member alone knows what is best for the citizens of Providence.[1]

Of course, the Providence Journal itself felt quite differently about the contract between the city and the library. In an op-ed appearing a few days later entitled "Peace at the Library," the Journal's board offered its congratulations to the PPL board and to the city officials, especially Mayor David Cicilline, for settling on an agreement that "over time, should substantially improve the ability of the library to provide services."[2]

After the contract was signed, it was discovered that although the jobs of seven children's specialists working at the Fox Point, Smith Hill, Olneyville, South Providence, and Wanskuck branches had been threatened by the Library, who had claimed poverty, PPL had the necessary funds after all.[3] On learning this, the Library Reform Group recommended to the City Council that the $250,000 the city had contributed to PPL be used for these child specialists' salaries rather than chucked into the pension fund as PPL had planned. Thankfully, the City agreed to lean on PPL to do this, and the jobs were preserved, at least for a little while.

The Library Partnership Advisory Committee

IN SEPTEMBER, THE LONG-AWAITED SIXTEEN-MEMBER BOARD OF THE Library Partnership Advisory Committee took shape. It was to be

---

1 Editorial, Linda Kushner, "Deal between Library and city is flawed" *Providence Journal* (June 21, 2007).

2 Editorial, "Peace at the library," *Providence Journal* (June 23, 2007).

3 PPL had the habit of projecting deficits that ultimately did not materialize as seen in the 990 tax returns.

co-chaired by Lisa Churchville, the president of PPL's board of trustees, and Kas DeCarvahlo, the mayor's representative on the PPL board. Other PPL members on the committee included Rob Taylor, Jauna Horton, and Oliver Bennett, as well as Mark McKenney (the governor's representative on the PPL board). The city was represented by John Simmons (the mayor's chief of administration) and Alan Sepe (the city's acting director of public property). Sharon Contreras represented the Providence Public School Department. But most importantly, there were members representing the public. The mayor appointed Myrth York, a former legislator who had run for governor, and Vicki Veh. Neither Myrth nor Vicki had been active in the reform movement, but both of them were strong supporters of library services and favored opening up the PPL. The city council cut right to the chase and appointed four Library Reform Group members who had been in the thick of the fight to reform PPL: Patricia Raub, Ellen Schwartz, Rochelle Lee, and Althea Graves. The Advisory Committee was charged with overseeing finances across the library system, but of course, they had no actual authority over the actions of the PPL trustees.

Those poor people, in my opinion, were now engaged in endless meetings and yet were powerless to affect the decisions of PPL. Although the committee's reports would be a regular standing agenda item at all PPL Board and PPL executive committee meetings, there was little indication that the committee's findings or recommendations would become factors in PPL decision-making. The memorandum of understanding that set out the work of the Advisory Committee in the Agreement for FY 08 clearly stated, "The parties recognize that the Committee's functioning is solely advisory."

You may, by now, recognize the cyclical nature of the problem of reforming the Library. We wanted a PPL board that would prioritize running a responsive library instead of an institution fixed on growing its endowment. PPL would not consider using what it called its endowment (but what was, in truth, a combination of donor-endowed funds and savings, which the board labeled endowment) to deal with emergency repairs or operating shortfalls. Rather, it engaged in a never-ending cycle of increased demands for municipal support while offering fewer services. No sooner would a contract be signed in late June or even in July (after the start of the fiscal year on July 1st), then PPL would announce that it needed more money and would threaten layoffs and/or branch closures in an effort to pressure the city to increase its library contribution in the budget for the next fiscal year.

In the spring of 2004, PPL had laid off twenty-one employees at Central and embarked on the unneeded modification of the building on Empire Street. In January 2005, they had suddenly closed the Washington branch. In the spring of 2006, PPL had announced that there was a $900,000 budget deficit and that it would have to lay off workers and close six of its ten branches. Even after Neil Steinberg pointed out that the deficit was only $500,000 and worked out a way for the city and PPL to close that hole in 2007 PPL again announced that they would lay off seven child specialists. Now, at the start of 2008, they announced that if the city did not take over running the branch libraries, some of the branches would be "mothballed." The Library Reform Group had its work cut out just to force PPL to maintain the level of services at the branches that there had been before 2004, not to mention enlarging branch services to meet the growing needs of the community.

Selective Accounting

THANKS TO THE INVESTIGATIVE SKILLS OF ELLEN SCHWARTZ, WE DIS-covered that PPL used a method of accounting that showed a deficit in their operating budget rather than a surplus in the yearly balance. Ellen wrote letters to all the PPL Board members, which she cc'ed to the president of the city council, the chairman and members of the city's Finance Committee, the mayor's chief of staff Bill Simmons, and Neil Steinberg detailing PPL's financials through Feb. 28, 2007.[1] She pointed out that the eight-month financial statements showed a significant under reporting of income. PPL "is reporting eight months of expenses and comparing it to six months of income," she stated. "It's no surprise that they are showing a deficit." She went on to demonstrate that if the cash figures were modified to reflect eight months of income instead of having a $996,050 deficit, there would be a $484,646 surplus. On March 31, 2007, an exasperated Ellen again wrote, "I guess no one read my letter. The PPL financial reports are still misleading. Nine months of expenses are still being compared to less than nine months of income. Even Bill Gates would show a deficit!"

PPL was also misleading about its endowment. It lumped gifts and savings with legally endowed funds and then held the entire amount sacrosanct as though it was a legal endowment that could not be used for operating needs of any kind. This practice allowed them to duck building maintenance. We had already seen the closure of Washington Park in December 2006 because PPL had failed to make necessary repairs to its roof in a timely manner. Library advocates were concerned that PPL might be deliberately avoiding making repairs in order to hasten the closure of branches. They were worried that PPL might allow the Knight Memorial as well as the Smith Hill and Washington Park branch buildings to deteriorate to such an extent that the Board could throw up its collective hands and close the branches. Library reformers interviewed the staff at Knight Memorial in November 2007 and learned from them that the roof needed repair. There were leaks in the building damaging the historic plaster works on the ceiling; water was dripping into the mezzanine and the children's areas.[2]

PPL was so accustomed to going to the city for money to resolve

---

1 Letter to PPL Board from Ellen Schwartz dated April 4, 2007.
2 Mike Nickerson, a custodial engineer at PPL, informed us that some of the leaks were due to the fact that PPL had ignored recommendations to have the gutters cleaned.

any problem that they failed to use other available sources. For instance, as the Library Reform Group pointed out to the press, because the city and PPL had not expressly agreed to reopen the Washington Park branch in the former firehouse, its home of fifty years, PPL lost the opportunity to apply for $100,000 in state historic preservation money for the needed repairs. Now, they seemed to be doing the same thing with Knight Memorial. Although the Library Reform Group had no power since they did not own the building, they contacted the head of the Providence Preservation Society to see whether Knight, a magnificent classical building built in 1924 as well as Washington Park, might be eligible to receive grant money from the Society to make the necessary repairs to preserve them. They communicated this idea to some PPL board members, but nothing came of it.

2008

THE BEGINNING OF 2008 BROUGHT NO CHANGE. ON JANUARY 9TH, despite the infusion of $250,000 extra city bucks in the FY 08 contract, which was designed to halt the firing of the child specialists from the branches, PPL announced that they would be laying off the seven child specialists in March unless further "additional money can be found to retain them."[1]

Child specialists were particularly needed in the small branches situated in the more impoverished neighborhoods. Neighborhood youth, who were encouraged to use the branches as safe places to come after school, needed the support of these librarians with their homework. PPL's firing of child specialists at this time made no sense. The Library had just hired five new librarians. An indignant Karen

1 Daniel Barbarisi, "The budget crunch – Library considers laying off seven child specialists," *Providence Journal* (January 9, 2008).

McAninch, the union representative, asked, "Why are we hiring people if we know we're going to be laying people off? It's a deliberate attempt to use the children's specialists as fodder.... In reality, when you come down to it, the children's specialists should have priority. They have been there longer."[2] Although PPL officials protested that the firing of children specialists did not mean they would be closing the branches, we reformers knew better. Today, they were reducing the service offered to their neediest users. Tomorrow, we were sure, the branches themselves would be on the chopping block.

Part of PPL's financial problem was the result of its negligent fundraising. Fundraising is a primary responsibility of all non-profit boards, and donated gifts and grants are a major source of income for private non-profit institutions. PPL had become so accustomed to going to the city for any money they needed that they had practically stopped fundraising. The annual reports of 2003-2003 showed $2,767,900 in contributions and non-governmental grants.[3] It included a wide range of contributors. My husband and I contributed, although since we only contributed $100, our donation as well as all those who gave less than $250 were not listed. By contrast, the FY 07 annual report shows only $1,179,925 in donations. The decline in non-governmental support was startling. Granted some of the donations in FY 03 were connected with capital campaigns associated with the renovation of Rochambeau and the South Providence branches, but this does not account for the stellar decline.

Neil Steinberg noted in his 2006 report that PPL's failure to fundraise contributed to the deficit. Recommendation #6 stated, "PPL will make a best effort attempt to resurrect annual fundraising to reduce

---

2   Daniel Barbarisi, "The budget crunch – Library considers laying off seven child specialists," *Providence Journal* (January 9, 2008).

3   Interestingly, the eight pages of listed contributions of between $250,000 and $250 total $4,530,250. In addition, there were two $1,000,000 grants which were not included in the above total.

the deficit and corresponding need for additional funding."[1] The Library Advisory Committee was quick to recommend that PPL get cracking on fundraising. They noted that PPL had not, like other major non-profits, held an annual fundraising event for three years.

The Library Reform Group took steps to shame and stimulate PPL to engage in more active fundraising. In February, we brought Louise Blalock, the chief librarian of the Hartford Connecticut Public Library, and Catherine Taylor, executive director of Westerly Rhode Island Public Libraries (both of whom had been very successful in raising money), to speak at a public meeting at Knight Memorial. We wanted to show that some libraries, even during difficult times, had expanded and improved library services. These admonishments had some effect. PPL actually began to turn its attention to fundraising. One board member, Kimberly Sutton, was interested in holding a large fundraising event. But to my knowledge, no event was held that year.

The Library continued to state that they were operating at a deficit. In August, the board announced, "Even if the city increased its annual contribution from $3.3 million to $3.4 million, it faces a $1.38 million deficit in its $9.7 million budget for this year."[2] The problem, they claimed, was that the library, with its branch system of nine branches, was unsustainable.

PPL's judgment of whether there were sufficient funds available to run the library and its branches was determined by its priorities. The trustees appeared to us reformers to be more concerned with growing the "endowment" of the institution than with creating funds to operate a library system complete with branches As Ellen Schwartz pointed out to the city council (and anyone else who would listen), PPL was depositing all its donations into the PPL Foundation.

1 Neil D. Steinberg "Providence Public Library Review," p. 8.
2 Daniel Barbarisi, "Refurbished library awaits council action – The Washington Park branch has been renovated but won't open until a pact is approved," *Providence Journal* (August 22, 2008).

There, the funds were treated as if they were part of the endowment, allowing only the interest to be spent for operating functions. As Ellen so clearly explained, "If a donor gives $100 to PPL, only $6 is considered part of the operating budget, and none of it is considered branch income." No wonder there was a deficit. Ellen suggested that all unrestricted donations should be placed into the current operating budget as donors had assumed would happen.

Also, PPL was taking money out of operating funds to pay its under-funded pension liability. Ellen suggested that PPL instead use some of the unrestricted funds that had been parked in the foundation to shore up the pension. Loss of future income would be balanced by lower pension costs in the future. "It's like paying off a mortgage," she explained, "You have less cash now, but you have to pay much less cash out in the future." But such a practice would reduce what PPL called its "endowment."

And, of course, prejudicing the case against the branches was the PPL's method of allocating its administrative costs, including the bloated salaries of its administrators. These administrative costs were above the national average for libraries. Ellen pointed out that PPL chose to use branch usage (the books taken out and reference questions answered at each branch) as the basis for allocating costs for the branches in their annual budget. This method resulted in two-thirds of the indirect cost of running the entire system ($1,187,300) being allocated to the branches. If PPL had chosen to allocate costs among the branches on the basis of the square footage of the branches, only forty-five percent of the costs ($830,340) would be allocated to the branches. If it had based the allocation on the number of employees working at the branches, less than one-third of the cost ($535,108) would be allocated to the branches. By using branch use as the metric for determining the portion of the budget necessary to run the branches, PPL was able to artificially inflate the cost of branch operations in order to demand a larger contribution from the city.

The concept of having a "sustainable library" had been floated by PPL for years. In 2006, you will remember, they had created the Strategic Planning Commission just to come up with the recommendation of a sustainable library system that was defined as the Central Library with three or four branches. The PPL Board was dominated by privileged businesspeople and/or persons who worked for their companies. Most of these people, who lived either outside Providence or in the affluent East Side neighborhood of the city, took pride in the elegant Central building that served as a resource center for the state. Their actions suggested only a grudging interest or understanding of the role the branches played across the city, including the opportunities the branches provided to otherwise underserved communities. The newly elected President of the Board of Trustees, Lisa Churchville, seemed to be especially enamored with New York's 42nd Street Library, a large central library that was separated from the extensive system of branches that served New York City's varied communities. She frequently raised this as an example of what PPL should look like, implying that the City of Providence could establish a department of library services to manage a branch system for the city.

The FY 2009 Contract

THE WRANGLING BETWEEN THE CITY AND THE LIBRARY CONTINUED past the start of the 2009 fiscal year. Finally, on July 17th, 2008, the library trustees agreed to a four-year contract. In return for the city paying PPL $3.5 million annually for four years, PPL would not close any branches in FY 2009. But it had six months to figure out what to do with the branches in the following year.[1] The contract stated that any branch closing or relocation starting July 1, 2009, must be announced by December 31, 2008. However, the city

---

1 Daniel Barbarisi, "Library agrees to 4-year pact with city," *Providence Journal* (July 18, 2008).

could push the closing back for a year if it was willing to pay the Library's projected operating deficit in 2009–2010. For this year, however, the library agreed to use $1.3 million from its endowment to plug the hole.

We library reformers saw this contract as a terrible move. It was now clear that PPL was intent on closing at least some of its branches. Their idea of sustainability meant branch closures. Mark McKenney, the governor's representative on the Board of Trustees, who was always concerned that the branches remained open, objected to the proposed contract. "This is a way for the city to give 'political cover' for libraries to close some of their branches," he said. "I think it is a mistake for us to pre-determine that a sustainable system is one with fewer branches."[2]

A news conference was hastily assembled by the Library Reform Group, together with the Friends groups of the Rochambeau, Smith Hill, and Mount Pleasant branches, and four city council members to point out the many flaws of the proposed contract. A major problem was the fact that the city would be obliged to pay the same amount each year no matter what level of library services were offered. But despite these flaws, the contract had its first passage through the city council.

The Reform group swung into action. We arranged for a press conference to be held one week later on July 24th at 5 o'clock in front of the former Washington Park branch library and notified the press and members of the library advocate groups to be there. By this time, we were raucously clear about our message. Reaching out to other groups who supported us, we urged them to join us in getting Providence residents to call the mayor's office and demand that he "go back to the drawing board and fix the flawed Library agreement."

The press conference was broadly covered. The *ProJo* reported

2 Daniel Barbarisi, "Library agrees to 4-year pact with city," *Providence Journal* (July 18, 2008).

that "the Board of Trustees for the Providence Public Library came under fire last night by more than two dozen critics for its failure to reopen the Washington Park branch."[1] Library critics also derided a proposed contract between PPL and the city that would commit the city to giving $3.5 million annually for the next four years, even if the board decided to cut services at the neighborhood branches in the following years. Councilors John Lombardy, Luis Aponte, Nicolas Narducci, and Miguel Luna told the assembled crowd that they opposed the contract as proposed and would vote to ratify it only if it were amended. They explained that an escape clause needed to be added that would allow the city to refuse to make annual payments if the trustees decided the only way to operate a sustainable system was to close the branches. Representative Aponte said there were enough votes on the city council to insist that the Washington Park branch, which had been closed by trustees since January 2006, be opened immediately. I added what we all had been thinking for years. "It is clear that it's the Library's $30 million endowment that the trustees want to sustain, not the library system itself."[2, 3]

Our press conference and the campaign of phone calls and letters

---

1 Richard C. Dujardin, "Critics demand reopening of library branches," Providence Journal (July 25, 2008).
2 Richard C. Dujardin, "Critics demand reopening of library branches," Providence Journal (July 25, 2008).
3 The devotion of PPL Trustees to the endowment was also noted by Maria DeCarvalho, the facilitator of the Municipal Working Group. "I always felt like they (PPL Board Trustees) felt so responsible for the endowment that [it] would be the measure of their service to the library. The measure of their failure or success [as a board member] would be whether they were able to maintain the integrity of their endowment" Interview of Maria DeCarvalho with Patricia Raub. "Saving Providence Public Library: Financial Crises and Community Activism." December 2021.

to the mayor's office had an immediate effect. One week later, PPL and the mayor's negotiators agreed to add an escape clause to the library agreement so that the city could withdraw from the four-year contract next June if the city officials were dissatisfied with PPL's plans for FY 09.

The Formation of the Providence Community Library (PCL)

ALTHOUGH THE SLIGHTLY AMENDED CONTRACT WAS NOT RATIFIED by the city until November 2008, it was clear as early as the end of August that the nine branches were in trouble. PPL was on the brink of jettisoning most, if not all, of branch libraries. We had tried for four years to reform PPL, but that had not worked. At the end of August, the Library Reform Group met, and I suggested that the time had come for us to create a new entity that could run the libraries for Providence. Reformers had toyed before with the idea of starting a new library, but it always seemed a pipe dream. Now, we felt there was no alternative: we had to prepare for the worst. The group approved the idea, and shortly after that, Patricia Raub, Marcus Mitchell, Ellen Schwartz, and I began to meet around my dining room table to form a non-profit that could, if necessary, run the libraries.

As with the formation of the Library Reform Group, the four of us brought different but complementary expertise to the enterprise. Ellen and I offered accounting and legal skills. Patricia, who had been the spokesperson for the Reform Group for four years and who had served on all kinds of library committees, brought this invaluable experience to the table. Marcus, as a business consultant, brought entrepreneurial experience to the mix. I thought of us as the four wheels of the enterprise that drove the project forward.

But there was also a fifth member of the group that formed PCL:

Karen McAninch, the union representative. The five of us were all in agreement that Providence needed a new entity to run its library system, but we came at it from different perspectives. Patricia, Ellen, Marcus, and I were most concerned with saving the nine branches. Karen was most concerned with saving the jobs of the library workers she represented. Sometimes, since she actually knew the most about the workings of a library, Karen was our steering wheel. But at other times, because she was coming from another place, she seemed to be taking off on her own path. Ultimately, Karen contributed the much-needed guidance on how to advance our goal of saving the nine branches without hurting the employees.

To create a non-profit corporation in Rhode Island, one must file articles of incorporation with the Secretary of State setting forth the name of the corporation, its purpose, its registered address, the name of the agent for the corporation, and the names of the initial board of directors. For financial purposes, we needed to establish a bank account, get a federal tax identification number, and apply for a 501(c)(3) tax exemption number. We also needed to develop the by-laws outlining the structures and operation of our organization, which would be adopted at its first full board meeting. But before doing these tasks, we had to answer a basic question: what would be the relation between the nine libraries?

Answering these questions took weeks. I remember looking out the window during one of these meetings and discovering that a cardinal was visiting the arborvitae that grew just outside. At the following meetings, watching the cardinal was my escape as we debated the nature and structure of our new library system.

We were determined that our library, with its nine neighborhood libraries, would not be modeled on PPL, which had a fully financed main library with far undersupported subsidiary branches. We could have easily followed PPL's model since one of the nine branches, Rochambeau, was by far the most active and richly endowed of the branches. But we wanted each neighborhood library to have the respect of an independent library yet work together with the other libraries as a unified library system. To that end, we immediately banned the use of the word "branch" in our system. It was amazingly hard to remove the word branch from our vocabulary after so many years of usage.[1] We also agreed that should any branches be shut down by PPL and consequently become part of our system, we would continue to employ the staff that had worked in those libraries.

But what should we name this library system we were creating? We knew that we were establishing a library system for Providence. And the factor that would most distinguish this library system was its communal nature. Community involvement and control were central to our mission. So, we fairly quickly settled on the words "Providence" and "community." But should it be "library" or "libraries?" To emphasize the unity of the system, we settled on Providence Community Library (PCL). However, I always had a problem with the word "library," which did not reflect the individuality and equality of the separate libraries. Recently, in 2022, after thirteen years of existence, PCL decided to rename itself. It is now known as the Community Libraries of Providence, (CLPVD) a name which I think much more accurately reflects the structure and nature of the library system we created.

Since it was not clear that we would actually have to step in and run any libraries for the city of Providence, we stated the purpose of the corporation was "to promote, support, organize and or manage a public library system in and for the city of Providence for the benefit of the community."[2]

The next question was who should head this new entity. There was no question that Patricia, Ellen, and I had done the yeoman's work to get us to this point. But Marcus offered certain advantages.

---

1 At the first meeting of the PCL board, we collected a dollar any time a PCL board member used the word "branch" to identify one of the nine libraries. We raised over $20 dollars.

2 Article of incorporation. Filing #200837258320 October 31, 2008

First, as Patricia pointed out, he was relatively unknown. He had just moved to Providence from Pennsylvania in 2006 and had immediately become active in the Rochambeau Friends and other organizations in the state. He became part of the Library Reform Group at the end of 2007. In contrast, Patricia, Ellen, and I were well-known quantities. Too well known. We were women who had been demanding change for years, and we had shown no hesitation in letting PPL know that we thought its priorities were wrong and its administration even worse. Marcus was different. He had a very calm demeanor, and his low male voice had gravitas. He had an amazing ability to summarize the main points of a meeting and bring people together. No matter how fractious a meeting became, he remained calm. And as Ellen, who herself favored T-shirts and jeans for every occasion, pointed out, "Marcus really filled a suit well."

It was decided that Marcus would be the president of the corporation as well as its spokesperson. Patricia would be the vice president. Ellen was the obvious choice for Treasurer. And I, who heretofore had only served as the president or an activist member of any organization I had belonged to, became the secretary.

The by-laws were harder to write. One thing we knew was that we did not want to be like PPL. That ultimately led to both the strengths and the weaknesses of our organization. We knew what was wrong with PPL, but how would we enshrine our radically new values in the structure of the organization and yet have an institution that functioned?

Primary to our endeavor was that the library be centered around the needs of the community. Neighborhood input, public representation, and residency were core issues to us. To that end, we created a board that was dominated by direct community representation. After much discussion, we settled on a board of up to twenty-five members, eighty percent of whom (not including the governor's representative) had to be Providence residents. The board also had to include members who lived in the catchment area of the nine branches of the library. To do this, we decided that the core of the Board would be nine members elected by and representing the Friends Groups of the nine branches. (This, of course, gave us the immediate challenge of developing new Friends Groups for the five branches that did not already have Friends Groups in existence.) The mayor would be entitled to appoint two representatives to the Board, the city council to appoint two members, and the governor of Rhode Island to appoint his representative. Most novel, the library employees would elect one of their own to serve on the board. Then, nine general members were to be elected by the board at each annual meeting. Concerned about the inordinately long time PPL members served (many for life), terms on PCL's board were limited to two years and for no more than three consecutive full terms.

The organization had four officers: president, vice president, secretary, and treasurer. The by-laws established four committees: finance, development, personnel, and facilities. The chairs of these committees, along with the mayor's staff appointee and the four officers of the organization, served as an executive committee. Regular board meetings were to be held monthly, except for August. All meetings were subject to the open meetings law, and an annual meeting would be held each September.

Having done all this work more or less in secret, we were set. We signed the Articles of Incorporation, and I quietly filed them at the office of the Secretary of State on October 31, 2008. Now, we waited for PPL to take its next step.

That did not take too long. At a Board meeting on December 18th, PPL announced that in July 2009, they planned to close the Fox Point, Smith Hill, Olneyville, Wanskuck, and Washington Park branches.[1] Only the downtown flagship and four other branches were to remain open. The branches that PPL had put on the chopping block were,

---

1 Philip Marcelo, "New Library plan would close City branches," *Providence Journal* (December 19, 2008).

of course, for the most part, located in the most underserved parts of the city, communities with the lowest income and the greatest percentage of Black and brown residents.

The vote on December 18th to close the five branches was ten to one. Mark McKenney, the governor's representative, was the only vote against it. The mayor's representative on the board, Kas DeCarvalho, had supported the library's plan to close the five branches with his abstention. Kas explained that his abstention was based on the caveat that the branches be returned to the city's possession to be run as neighborhood learning centers for after-school activities, public computer access, and meeting space.[1]

We were horrified but not surprised. At that point in the meeting, Marcus Mitchel rose and, using his two-minute public comment, stated, "The Board's plan is unacceptable. The library is asking the city for funding to provide library services when their plan proposes a severe reduction in service that will adversely affect the community."[2] He then informed the meeting that we, a coalition of library groups, had formed a new nonprofit, the Providence Community Library, and that we stood ready to run the city's libraries. The announcement was dynamite.

The next day, notwithstanding the vote of his own representative on the board, the mayor did a turnaround and announced that he opposed Providence Public Library's proposal to close five neighborhood branches. Trying to control the problem, he stated, "As I have made clear for many years, I am opposed to any plan that reduces the presence of library services in our neighborhoods. I understand the financial difficulties of administering a large, public institution, especially in these times, but it's critical that we uphold the hundred-year-old mission of the Providence public library for today and for

---

1   Philip Marcelo, "In a shift, Cicilline wants to retain library branches," *Providence Journal* (December 20, 2008).

2   Phillip Marcelo, "New library plan would close five city libraries," *Providence Journal* (December 19, 2008).

the future." Kas was quick to state that the mayor's statement did not contradict how he, Kas, had characterized Cicilline's position at the PPL board meeting. "The mayor is willing to look at anything so long as it involves the same services provided as the branch system. The mayor's primary interest with respect to the library branches is in maximizing services." So, where was the mayor on this issue?

To understand just how crazy and erratic PPL's actions were, the Library announced that the reopening of Washington Park was imminent. The branch, which had sat closed for two years, was to reopen in its old home within a month notwithstanding the fact that PPL was planning to permanently close it down less than six months later. Of course, the actual opening did not occur until the end of March 2009, four months later than it needed to have been. By December 08, to the tune of $400,000, the city had fixed the roof, serviced the boiler, installed a new fire alarm system, realigned the gutters, painted the walls, installed carpet and painted the exterior, and repainted some of the brick exterior of the old firehouse in Washington Park. The building was just about ready for use as a library, but to the consternation of the community, the refurbished building sat empty while PPL and the city continued to wrangle. The city was intent on holding off several weeks of work still needed until a lease was signed, demonstrating that the library would definitely reopen. Meanwhile, PPL did nothing to install the needed books and furniture. In December 2008, we joined with city councilors and Washington Park community leaders to point out the stupidity and cruelty of the situation. But it was not until March 26, 2009, that the Washington Park branch was finally opened. At that time, we learned that because PPL had stored Washington Park's book collections in leaky and humid sheds behind Knight Memorial, the branch lost many books of particular interest to the local community. "We lost a lot of our adult fiction and nonfiction. We had a really strong Civil Rights and African American history collection that we lost a part of, and we still don't have a strong Spanish language section, which is really important to develop for this neighborhood," said Washington Park librarian Lanham Bundy.[1] Now, PPL was scheduling this newly opened and refurbished library to be closed in just three months!

Jan-May 2009: The Rush to Get the Contract

FOR YEARS, PPL HAD LEVERAGED THE THREAT THAT THE CITY MIGHT have to create a library department to run its libraries to demand more and more municipal money to run its shrinking library system. But now the jig was up. There was a new non-profit in town willing to take over the job of running the libraries.

Following Marcus's revelation at the December 18, 2009, PPL Board meeting that we reformers had created a 501(c)(3), the Providence Community Library, and that we were willing to run the city's libraries, we launched a campaign to win the city's contract to run the libraries. Marcus called on the city to transfer library funding from PPL to PCL, which he said would ensure continued access to a nine-branch library system and provide services and programs that meet the needs of library patrons across a city."[2]

On January 6th, Marcus outlined the structure of PCL to the press.[3] Ellen, our financial wizard, explained that PCL could save the city more than $2,000,000 a year. Rob Taylor, the vice President of PPL's Board of Trustees, had informed us that the cost of operating the nine branches was $7.5 million of the total $9.7 million operating budget

---

1 Philip Marcelo, "Washington Park Library Reopens After Major Renovations," *Providence Journal* (March 27, 2009).

2 Philip Marcelo, "New group wants to run city branches," *Providence Journal* (Jan 5,2009).

3 Philip Marcelo, "Library savings, quality pledged," *Providence Journal* (January 6, 2009).

Picture of founders (left to right) Linda J. Kushner, Patricia Raub, Karen McAninch, Marcus Mitchell, missing Ellen Schwartz. In front of Smith Hill Library. February 2009. Providence Business News

of PPL.[4] Ellen announced that PCL's proposed operating budget for FY 2010 was $4.8 million to run the nine branches.[5]

The ProJo reported that PCL already had the support of nine of the fifteen city counselors. With a $3000 grant from the city council, we hired Louise Blalock, who had been the director of the Hartford Public Library for seventeen years, as our consultant to develop a five-year budget to run the nine branches. The council grant was a godsend since PCL, unlike PPL, did not have an endowment. In fact,

---

4 Philip Marcelo, "Library savings, quality pledged," *Providence Journal* (January 6, 2009).

5 Philip Marcelo, "Library savings, quality pledged," *Providence Journal* (January 6, 2009).

it had no money of its own. From time to time, I and others covered small expenses, but we needed this grant just as we needed the mayor to choose us over the PPL.

Winning the contract for the libraries required that we play both an "inside" and "outside" game. The inside game was to convince Mayor David Cicilline that we had the ability to run a library system. I remembered all too clearly a meeting we had with David a few years earlier, possibly in 2007. We had been urging the mayor to join with the city council to force PPL to add publicly appointed members to its board as a condition of receiving city money. Suddenly, almost out of nowhere, the mayor, who I knew personally, exclaimed, "What! You mean you would have Linda Kushner run the libraries!" I was surprised and astonished that he would suggest such a thing. Certainly, as determined as we were to improve the libraries, we hadn't yet thought of creating a new non-profit to run them. "No," I replied to the mayor, "We don't want to run the libraries; we just wanted PPL to do a better job of running them for the city's residents." And I added, "I assure you, David, that should I ever find myself charged with running the libraries, I would certainly hire professional librarians to do it—including a new library director to do a better job than Dale Thompson is doing!"

But now we had reached the point of creating a new library system to supplant PPL. All attempts at reforming PPL had certainly failed. We had created a nonprofit to do the job. But we still had to convince the mayor that having studied all aspects of running a library -financial, personnel, technical services, facilities, programs—PCL was capable of managing Providence's libraries. Although the mayor would ultimately change his position and support PCL running the branch libraries, his doing so was certainly not a foregone conclusion. As David had expressed numerous times, he was reluctant to abandon a 138-year-old institution that, for better or worse, had provided Providence with its library services.

Negotiating With the City

FEEDING AN UNENDING STREAM OF QUARTERS INTO VORACIOUS PARKING meters on Washington Street, we headed off to repeated meetings at City Hall with the mayor's staff. There, we were grilled on how we, people with absolutely no experience in running a library, proposed to run an entire library system for New England's third-largest city. We brought with us our formal fourteen-page "Proposal to Transfer Branch Libraries to the Providence Community Library,"[1] which contained a description of the board structure of PCL, a projected budget for FY 09-10 (vetted by three urban Library directors from Rhode Island, Massachusetts, and Connecticut), the projected staffing of PCL for 2009-10, plans for addressing the maintenance of the buildings, and a comparison of costs between PPL and PCL. Attached to the report were letters of support from the Friends of Rochambeau Branch, Friends of the Wanskuck Branch Library, Fox Point Senior Citizens Inc., Mount Hope Neighborhood Association, The Fox Point Neighborhood Association, and The Brown/Fox Point Early Childhood Education Center.

The principal person who met with us was the mayor's director of operations, Alix Ogden. Alix's background was particularly apt for vetting us. Before joining the mayor's staff, Alix had served as the director of the city's park department. During her tenure, the city had entered into a contract with the RI Zoological Society, a non-profit 501(c)(3), to support and maintain the city's zoo at Roger Williams Park. Alix had the experience of working with a private non-profit corporation that supported and maintained a municipal asset for the city's parks, just as PCL hoped to do for the city's libraries.

Over four months of meetings in the mayor's offices, we fielded a

---

1 M. Mitchell, P. Raub, L.J.Kushner & E. Schwartz, "Proposal to Transfer Branch Libraries to the Providence Community Library," (January 2009). Author's personal files.

stream of unending questions about the structure of our board, how many PPL employees would be retained at the branches, how we would obtain private funding, who would own the buildings, and most astonishing to the city, how would be able to run nine branches for less money than PPL said was possible. It seemed like we were being put through a wringer.

We met as a large group at least four times. Sometimes, we were accompanied by our lawyer, Jay Glasson, who discussed the legal implications of the transfer. It was great to have Jay there. With his no-nonsense approach, he helped set boundaries. He drew firm legal limitations to contain our desperate willingness to do almost anything to obtain the City contract. I had gone to see Jay in early 2008 to ask his advice. He had thought we were crazy. "I thought they had good intentions, but there was no way they could do it. PPL was an established institution. It's like paddling a canoe against the tide," he later told me when I interviewed him in preparation for writing this book. I returned to see Jay in October 2008. By then, PPL had given notice that they were planning to close five libraries, and we were secretly creating a non-profit corporation to run the five libraries if necessary. This time, Ellen and Patricia joined me to plead to Jay that he take our case. Even though he still thought we were crazy, he agreed to help us, pro bono, of course! Clearly, we had no money.

Jay immediately brought a needed dose of reality. "You don't know what you are getting into," he told us. And he was right! The buildings—except Rochambeau and South Providence, which had recently been renovated—were a disaster. Washington Park had been closed because it was "unsafe." Library patrons at Knight Memorial, Smith Hill, and Wanskuck had to dodge around buckets on rainy days. And these were just some of the most visible problems. "You need to know the entire scope of the problems," he said, and advised us to hire a structural engineer to find out what other problems existed before entering into any contract with the city. We did not listen to him, and perhaps this naivety is what enabled us to push through with our dream.

He wisely argued that we not assume responsibility for paying for the repair of the buildings. Either PPL, who owned the buildings, or the city, who would lease them, should have the responsibility for fixing them. Things were so complex that in February, when we were actually vying with PPL for the city's contract, Jay advised us to ask the city for a six-month transition period and take over the libraries on September 1, 2009. For us, this was not an option. PPL had made it crystal clear that they were not interested in running the branches after June 30th, and we were absolutely determined that all the branches would stay open.

Jay was also concerned that PCL received some portion of the endowment. He, like me, had done some preliminary research and found cases that gave us standing. Clearly, not all of the donations to the "endowment" had been given with only the central library in mind. Many East Side residents, who had made significant donations to PPL, were active patrons of the Rochambeau branch and considered it "their library." Some of their donations had surely been made with Rochambeau in mind. The Knight Memorial Library turned over its endowment to PPL when it became part of the PPL system in 1962. Clearly, the donors to Knight Memorial, before it became part of PPL, had donated to support the Knight Memorial Library and not PPL's central library. Jay thought some of these donors could bring a suit against the PPL Foundation to claw back some of the donations and have them used for the branches. But in the rush to get the contract with the city and work out the physical and personnel changes necessary for the transfer, we delayed dealing with the issue of the endowment.[1]

---

1 After the transfer of the library contract to PCL, on July 1, 2009, we tried to get the Tavares administration to pursue the endowment issue. But for some reason, perhaps because they were busy fighting to get the library buildings transferred to the City, the city solicitor let the endowment issue go by the wayside. PCL did manage to obtain a portion of the endowment which had been raised by the Knight Memorial Library prior to its joining PPL transferred to it.

Ellen carried the lion's share of explaining how we could operate the nine branches for less than $4.9 million. The actual proposal we submitted to the city set revenue at $4,800,169: $3,500,000 from the city of Providence, $750,000 from the state of Rhode Island in grants in aid, and $550,169 to be raised by PCL in donations and grants and from fines and fees. My job was to convince the city that we could and would be able to raise the $500,000 plus. You will remember that PPL, an established institution, had failed miserably in fundraising. It had only raised $429,000 in the fiscal year ending June 30, 2009. I knew nothing about fundraising for a non-profit, but I wasn't afraid to try. The only experience I had with raising money was for my Senate campaign in 1992. That had taught me one thing. If you want to get money, you have to ask for it. And ask all the time.

But to get professional advice, I spoke with Steve Sorin, who was the development director at Trinity Repertory Theater from 1996-2009. Steve had developed a robust fundraising effort. Anchored by a number of significant donations above $50,000 and with a broad general appeal, the company raised $1.8 million a year. I asked Steve if he thought a non-profit with the broad purpose of providing library services to the city's communities could raise $500,000. He gave me a resounding yes. Neil Steinberg of the Rhode Island Foundation was more cautious. At a meeting in early 2009, he told Ellen Schwartz and me that an organization's success in fundraising depends to a large extent on the magnetism of its director. A strong director with a big personality pulls money in. That was certainly true of Trinity, which had been led by such exuberant directors as Adrian Hall and Oskar Eustis and now was under the direction of the outgoing and engaging Curt Columbus. Who knew what Director we would have?

Most helpful in convincing the city that we could raise the needed funds was David Karloff, a former Vice President for Grant-making at the Rhode Foundation, who joined our transition team and, with his experience, vetted our figures for the city. Louise Blalock, the director of the Hartford Connecticut Public Library, who had helped us develop our budget, came with us to some of the meetings to vouch for the accuracy and adequacy of our numbers to run the city's libraries.

In a community as closely knit as Providence, the mayor's office was particularly concerned that library employees were not hurt by the transfer from PPL to PCL. Clearly, that was also our goal. Our proposal was premised on keeping the fifty union employees presently employed at the branches in the same jobs at their contractual salaries and employing eight nonunion library administrative staff, most of whom were already library employees. Karen McAninch, the union representative of the Library's staff, went with us to the meetings and fielded the personnel issues and other practical questions flung at us by the city officials.

It seemed that the city had it in for us, but as Alix explained to me when I interviewed her for this book, they were just doing due diligence to ensure that our 501(c)(3) had the infrastructure necessary to support our mission of running the libraries. Alix assured me that her deep involvement in this process was because the mayor actually wanted to have the option of choosing us.[1] But this certainly wasn't clear to us at that time.

One change the mayor's office demanded of the PCL's by-laws was that one of the two representatives on the board picked by the mayor should specifically be a member of his administration and not just a member of the public. We recognized that this was a great idea. Not only would it involve the mayor's office more directly in board decisions, but conversely, it would make library concerns more central to the mayor. We agreed to the change immediately.

Among the questions that plagued us was what did it mean when branch libraries were "turned over" to the PCL. Did that include the furniture, the books, and fixtures like the phones and computers that were in the branches? And to whom were they turned over?

---

1 Personal interview with Alix Ogden, March 1, 2023.

This was particularly critical as to the ownership of the buildings. In 2009, PPL owned the buildings housing seven of the branches: Rochambeau, Mount Pleasant, Knight Memorial, Smith Hill, South Providence, Olneyville, and Wanskuck. The city owned the building housing the Washington Park branch. Space for the ninth branch, Fox Point, was rented from the Fox Point Boys and Girls Club. PCL did not want to own buildings. We were interested in managing the library, not owning it. However, we did not want to rent the buildings from PPL. We did not trust them. We wanted the Library to give the buildings to the city. This was not a far-fetched idea. As recently as Dec 18, 2008, the *Providence Journal* had reported that Rob Taylor, the VP of PPL's Board, had said: "that the library had told the city it was willing to donate the branch buildings and their contents (books, computers, furnishings,) to the city." [1] But now, would PPL actually step up to the plate and transfer the branches to the city? The answer was "no!"

There were also questions about who, the city or PCL, would have the responsibility to repair and/ or pay for timely and needed repairs to the buildings. And how would our being the managers versus the owners affect our ability to apply for grants to repair these buildings?

Winning the Support of the Community

MEANWHILE, LIBRARY REFORM ADVOCATES WERE ALSO BUSY WITH THE "outside game," that of getting the community to push the city to award us the contract to manage the branches to PCL. Everyone had a date with their Rolodexes—each advocate pulling in their special contacts to pressure the city to transfer the branch libraries. Rochelle Lee turned to her contacts in the arts community, bringing in the

---

1   Philip Marcelo, "New Library Plan Would Close 5 Branches," *Providence Journal* (December 19, 2008)

support of Valarie Tutson and Len Cabral of the Black Storytellers centered in South Providence and drawing on the expertise of Bert Crenca, who had helmed the development of AS220, the fast-growing alternative arts organization in Providence. Patricia drew on her history of working with the many groups that were springing up in support of the libraries. Ellen worked on her client list.

I went through lists of all the people who had supported my campaign for the U.S. Senate in 1992, as well as every union leader and every political operative I could think of. I also decided to contact the directors of community centers in Providence. I first called them because I thought that since they ran programs for children in underserved areas, they might be especially concerned with the loss of library services. But John DeLuca, the director of the Charles Street DaVinci Center, opened my eyes to the huge service the branch libraries provided to adults in these communities. With the advent and spread of computers, many jobs could now only be applied for on the computer. However, many people in Providence did not have computers. These people were completely dependent on the computers in the branches (as well as the assistance of the librarians there) to apply for jobs. But John explained to me that the need to use the branches' computers was even more basic. Not only did one have to have a computer to apply for a job, but a person also needed a computer to apply for benefits, including unemployment benefits and food stamps.

In January and February, we set up and publicized public forums at all eight of the operating branches to alert the public to PPL's plan to close five branches and to inform library users of our competing plan to continue library service at all nine branches. PPL administrators and PCL founders faced off before large audiences of library patrons. Patricia, Ellen, Marcus, and I each represented PCL at different forums. Generally, the forums were civil, even friendly affairs, with each side presenting its points. But at a forum at the Rochambeau branch where Marcus and I were talking, an audience member stood up and intimated that Marcus was pushing PCL because Marcus would get a paying job out of it. Marcus, as usual, took the remark calmly. He asked the man to identify himself. The man said that he was "a member of the public." But Marcus had recognized the man as Frederick Buhler, the husband of Dale Thompson, PPL's over-paid Director. "Well, your intimations are certainly untrue," Marcus replied coolly, "and it is rich to hear it coming from you since you are Dale Thompson's husband who enjoys the more than $140,000 of mostly taxpayer money that your wife brings home."[1] There was a gasp and then a giggle in the audience.

We organized a letter-writing campaign to petition the mayor's office and the city council to transfer the city's contract from PPL to PCL. These forums helped. More than 1000 letters were sent.

Establishing Friends Groups

THE PCL BY-LAWS WE HAD WRITTEN IN SEPTEMBER CALLED FOR representatives on the board elected by each of the Friends Groups. But at this time, only three libraries—Rochambeau, Smith Hill, and Mt Pleasant—had Friends groups. Now, we had to create six new Friends Groups. Fox Point, you may remember, had just about formed a Friends group in 2004. But it had gone dormant when PPL Director Dale Thompson put the kibosh on it. Now facing possible extinction as one of the five branches scheduled for closure, the group sprung back into existence with an organizing meeting in April 2009.

I was always surprised that Knight Memorial Library did not have a Friends Group. It was one of the three "large" branches. In fact, it was much larger than the Rochambeau and Mt. Pleasant, the two other large libraries. Located in the Elmwood area of Providence, the library

---

1 Personal conversation with Marcus Mitchell June 22, 2023

had been started by a group of women who founded the Elmwood Public Library Association in 1915. Soon afterward, in 1924, one of the group's wealthier members encouraged her family, the Knights, to build a large, ornate, renaissance-style marble building to house the library's book collection. The Elmwood Association remained active in the management of the library until it was transferred to PPL in 1962. Although there was no formal support group for Knight in existence in 2008, there were sufficient neighborhood supporters to quickly form a Friends Group—especially since incredibly PPL was threatening to close their library, a focal place in the community.

The organization of the Olneyville Friends centered around Cynthia Wilmot. Cyndie, who was the chief of human resources for Lifespan's corporate sector, had become a part of the Olneyville Collaborative, a collection of non-profits who worked in the area. Hearing about a forum that was being held at the Olneyville branch to discuss the competing plans, Cyndie decided to go. Patricia and I also went.

Cyndie could not understand how PPL could be handing out a beautiful colored brochure picturing all the branches, including Olneyville, when PPL had decided to close it. She let the PPL representative at the meeting know in no uncertain terms what she thought of the ploy. When we saw this woman standing up to the PPL spokesperson, we knew she was our kind of person. As soon as the meeting was over, we sat down with Cyndie and asked her if she would help us start a Friends Group for the Olneyville branch. Cyndie was enthusiastic. She quickly rounded up a few people from the neighborhood who she thought would be interested in having a strong Olneyville library. A few meetings later, the Olneyville Friends Group was established. The group elected Cyndie as their representative on the PCL board. Washington Park's experience of having been shuttered for two years and now the threat of permanent closure had created a strong cohort of supporters. Under the leadership of Bob Medeiros and Sister Ann, the group easily metamorphosed into a Friend Group. The hardest library to form a Friends Group from was the South Providence branch. But with the continued work of Sister Ann, whose parish church, St Michael's, was just across the street, a group slowly materialized and was formally recognized as the South Providence Friends in 2010 after PCL was running the library.

Making Progress

GRADUALLY, THINGS BEGAN TO CHANGE. ON JANUARY 29, 2009, I opened the paper to find an editorial by the *Providence Journal* board entitled "A Library Lifeline?" It read: "An intriguing idea has arisen that would put the Providence Public Library's nine branches into the hands of a newly created nonprofit, leaving the PPL (also a nonprofit) in charge of the central branch—its heart and soul—on Empire Street. Although the proposal needs further vetting, it might be better than continuing the tenuous status quote or having the PPL shut down five branches and hand over four to the city to run as 'community learning centers."[1] Of course, true to form, the *Journal* stuck it to us: "We have no idea whether this concept is feasible, and especially whether those who make up the Providence Community Library would bring adequate management skills to overseeing some or all of the branches. And we wonder about its capacity to fend off powerful political pressures, especially given the proposed composition of its board. Still, this proposal, or a variant of it, might cut the Gordian knot of rival interests that have fought for control of the PPL and its finances for the last several years."[2] What a surprise!

Then, on April 2nd, the PPL Board of Trustees voted to work

---

1 Providence Journal editorial, "Editorial – A Library Lifeline," *Providence Journal* (January 29, 2009).
2 Providence Journal editorial, "Editorial – A Library Lifeline,"*Providence Journal* (January 29, 2009).

with the PCL to help it take over the branch libraries.[3] We were ecstatic. "The vote goes beyond just acknowledging us as a viable entity, but shows that PPL is looking for ways to support us," said a very optimistic Marcus Mitchell.[4]

Yet, it was still a hard decision for the mayor to make. How could he jettison an organization that had run the city's libraries for 138 years for a new organization run by four people, none of whom had any experience running a large non-profit, much less a library system?

Finally, on April 27th, we felt that we had done all we could, and it was time for the mayor to fish or cut bait. We sent him a letter politely demanding that he make a decision. We wrote:

As you know, the Providence Community Library has expended considerable time and money in an effort to provide the city of Providence with an alternative to the continually shrinking and unresponsive PPL. Starting last August, when we first thought of starting a nonprofit library organization, we have:
- Formed a Rhode Island corporation.
- Analyzed PPL's budget and determined the real cost of running a nine-branch library system.
- Consulted with library directors in Rhode Island, Massachusetts, and Connecticut.
- Developed a budget for PCL's operation of the nine branches.
- Developed by-laws that give the Friends Groups, the Mayor, the City Council, and the Governor, as well as a core steering committee, power to select members to serve on the governing board.

3 Philip Marcelo, "Providence Library May Transfer Branches to New Group," *Providence Journal* (April 3, 2009).

4 Philip Marcelo, "Main Library May Cede Branches," *Providence Journal* (April 4, 2009).

- Held informational forums at all the branches.
- Hired a professional library consultant to help us develop a five-year operating budget.
- Met repeatedly with PPL staff to learn of their concerns and hear their suggestions.
- Created a transition team equipped to deal with the library, legal, and real estate issues involved in transferring the management of the nine branches to PCL.
- Drafted, with the help of professional librarians and library school faculty, our long-range plan for a 21st-century library.
- Developed a fundraising plan and goal.
- Met informally with the Champlin Foundation, the Rhode Island Foundation, and United Way to keep them abreast of developments in the Providence library situation.
- Met with a number of individuals and corporate groups who have contributed to the support of the libraries.
- Helped library patrons establish Friends Groups, resulting in the formation of Friends Groups at all nine branches.
- Met with your staff to discuss some of the issues that need to be addressed to effect the transfer of the management of the branch library from PPL to PCL.
- Met with PPL representatives to discuss technical issues relating to providing library services at the branches.

All these actions were undertaken without any assurance that the city would indeed decide to use PCL to manage the branch libraries. But now, unfortunately, we have come to the point where we cannot do anymore without a letter from you, explicitly, informing us that PCL will be chosen by the city to manage the branch library systems.... July 1, as you know, is only two months away, and it is clear that as of that date, the branches will be closed, the central library will be partially closed, and the public will be in an uproar. We would ask that you send us a letter by April 30th so we can continue to do the job that needs to be done.1

The four of us, Marcus, Patricia, Ellen, and myself, each signed the letter and delivered it to the mayor's office. Then, for a few days, we did nothing!

On April 30th, we received a letter from the mayor stating that the city would enter into a contract with PCL to run the nine branch libraries starting on July 1st.[2] Yikes! July 1st was sixty-one days away!

Getting Ready for the Transfer

WHAT DO YOU THINK OF WHEN YOU THINK OF LIBRARIES? I IMAGINE that you think of books, the library clerk who checks out your books, and possibly the librarian who helps you find and/or place a reserve on a book you need for a paper. Maybe, since we are in the twenty-first century, you think about computers that occupy a part of every reading room. Perhaps you think of that quiet corner in your library where, from time to time, you escape from the world's demands. That is what I thought about.

I certainly did not know about the more than forty phones located in the nine branches, which were tied to a single internet system controlled by the central library. I certainly was not aware that more than three hundred computers were scattered across the branches, some for public use but most used by the staff to process the books, all of which computers were tied to the PPL domain.

---

1 Letter from Marcus Mitchell, Patricia Raub, Linda Kushner and Ellen Schwartz to Mayor David N. Cicilline, April 27, 2009. Copy in author's personal files.

2 Letter from Mayor David N. Cicilline to Marcus Mitchell president of the Providence Community Library, April 30, 2009.

I never thought about how a book became an actual library book. How does that book get from being published to sitting on the library shelf, ready for you to take out? I hardly knew that there was an entire department of eight employees at PPL called Technical Services whose job it was to order and enter books into the PPL system, giving each item its own number and entering it into the catalog. Now, we would need some of those employees to designate all the books at the branches as PCL books. I never thought about how books got from one library to another. What made it possible for me to reserve a book that was actually owned by the Cumberland or Newport Library and have it arrive at my branch ready for me to borrow? I was totally ignorant of the role of Ocean State Libraries. And, of course, while I sat in my comfy chair in the corner, I took the heat and electricity, not to mention the upkeep and repair of nine separate buildings, for granted. I did not realize we would have to bargain with PPL to have some of their maintenance staff become PCL employees.

The mayor's letter of April 30th triggered an almost impossible race to separate the two library systems in sixty-one days and to turn PCL into a fully functioning independent library system. Patricia, Ellen, Karen McAninch, and I went into high gear to make this possible. Sometimes, we worked in areas that were familiar to us—Ellen with finance, Karen with personnel—but at times, we found ourselves tangling with problems that, although foreign to us, needed to be solved if PCL were to come into existence as a fully functioning library system.

An immediate problem was money. We did not have an endowment to dip into. Aware of the costs of preparing the libraries for the transfer as well as the problem of covering some costs for the first month before the city money would come through, I wrote to Neil Steinberg, the head of the RI Foundation, asking for a grant of

$110,495 from the Foundation's discretionary funds.[1] I thought that because PCL was performing a vital community function affecting 1000s of people by keeping branch service available without interruption in the communities that needed it the most, and because it was a one-time grant, we might get the needed money. I also thought that because Neil had prepared "The Steinberg Report," he would be sympathetic to our efforts to provide library services. I was wrong. Sympathetic or not, the grant was not forthcoming. We just had to soldier through on our own.[2]

One of the problems concerned how we would contract for needed services. The heating company, the electric company, and various other vendors wanted a name of a person and a contact number for the services they would be providing to PCL. What to do? An easy answer, I thought. I would give them my name and number to use until we hired the business manager who would deal with these problems. I was banking on the city, making its first quarter payment on time. This was something they didn't usually do, but the administration knew it was essential for the PCL's takeover to work. So, out of an abundance of confidence, I did it. I gave them my name. I am very glad to report that Sue Gibbs, our wonderful business director, was one of our first hires and that the city came through with its first quarter payment on time. So, I never had to shell out to cover the gas and electricity needed for nine library buildings. But for years afterward, even with Sue in control, I occasionally got telephone calls from the utilities and various vendors for problems concerning the libraries. I immediately referred them to Sue, who quickly cleared up the matter.

Yet there was still a problem of immediate costs. Without a grant

1 Letter from Linda Kushner to Neil Steinberg. May 11, 2009. Copy in author's personal files.

2 PCL did receive a $25,000 grant from the Rhode Island Foundation in September 2009 after we took over the branches,

from the RI Foundation or an endowment, we had nothing to draw upon. And as Ellen so cogently pointed out, how could we stock the nine bathrooms with toilet paper while waiting for the city's first check? Crazy me. I knew that Ellen was meticulous in her budgeting and that the money would be there eventually to cover such expenses. So, I loaned PCL $50,000. I was confident that under Ellen's steward-ship, I would be fully repaid. And so I was. As soon as the city came through with its first payment, I was promptly repaid.

Deciding which PPL librarians, clerks, and child specialists would become PCL employees and who would remain with PPL was not that difficult. For the most part, the employees who were already based at the branches became PCL employees. But there were a few instances where personnel from downtown with seniority elected to come to PCL, starting off a series of job bumping. And there was one heartbreaking decision. Because we needed to run the nine branches with much less overhead than PPL did, we had to eliminate one regional librarian position. Our budget required that instead of having three regional librarians to administer the nine libraries, we would have to make do with two. Marcus took on the difficult job of informing one of the librarians that her position had been eliminated. He did it with as much heart and grace as was possible. But it was heart-wrenching.

Deciding how to staff the less visible parts of the library, Technical Services (who order and process the books), Information Technol-ogy (who manage our computers, phones, and web page), and the maintenance department (who maintain our nine buildings), was much more complex.

Tech Services at PPL had eight people: the head, two librarians, a head of the ordering department, a cataloging specialist, and three clerks. How many people did we need? And more importantly, how many could we afford? Also, where would we house this department, which had always been located downtown? There was some discus-sion about our paying PPL for the tech services needed to service the branches for a few months until we were up and running. But the charges that PPL demanded for this help were way beyond our budget. After careful consideration, we decided five of these people would leave PPL and become PCL employees.

But where would the tech service department be situated? Patricia and I went to various branches to check out the possibilities. Besides being the work area for up to five people, the area also needed to be sufficiently spacious and designed to receive and send out large deliveries of books. It needed a loading dock. Two places that looked possible, in that they had some empty rooms with access to a loading area, were Wanskuck and Mt. Pleasant. However, both these locations had to be rejected when we discovered that each of them had stairs that would have to be negotiated. We asked PPL if they might help us out by allowing our tech services people to continue working at the central library until Sept 1st to give us time to solve the housing problem. But PPL rejected this. Finally, we decided that we had to rent space for the department away from the libraries in a building on Manton Avenue. Ugh, now we were involved with ten locations.

Disentangling the forty-four telephones and the more than three hundred computers located in the branches from central servers at the downtown central library was a mammoth task. In fact, it was so huge that Tom O'Donnell, the regional librarian at Rochambeau, doubted it could be done without disrupting library services. "At this time," he wrote us, "I can't see the PCL (even with the full cooperation of PPL) being able to accomplish these and other of the technological aspects of the transition without a significant interruption of services. And I fear we may have to shut down for the summer just to get our technology in order! I hope I am wrong, but the branches can't function without phones and computers. If I am wrong and someone can show me otherwise, I would appreciate it."[1]

---

1 "A Couple of Concerns," memorandum from Tom O'Donnell. May 6, 2009. Copy in author's personal files.

OSL, the state Office of Library Services, suggested that we continue to stay connected to the PPL system for six months as they, too, believed that a transaction to separate systems could not take place before July 1st. But they did not count on the determination of the PCL founders. More importantly, they were unaware of the immense skill and drive of David Sok, a member of PPL's Information Technology department, who opted to become the head of our IT department.

PPL had employed four people in their Information Technology department. As the most recently hired person, David was the low man on the totem pole. He was certain he would be let go when the split took place. Although we were courting David to come to PCL and be our computer technology specialist, he was not sure he wanted to be part of PCL. As he later told me, he admired our enthusiasm and determination but did not think we had the experience necessary to run the library system. Like others, he was not sure we would last more than a year. He thought his layoff from PPL with its unemployment benefits might provide an opportunity for him to go back to school and get a higher degree in technology. David did not see libraries as the industry in which he wanted to work forever. But we persisted, and with much courting and an increase in the salary we were offering, David finally decided to join us. He was a godsend. As Deb Furia later described him to me, "David Sok not only knows everything, but he is also a penny-pincher with a soul." Just what we needed at PCL.

I ran into David at Rochambeau one day in June. He was hard at work reconfiguring one of the phones. There were more than forty telephones located in the nine branches. All of them were part of an internet phone system (Voice Over I.P.) controlled from the Central Library. David was working to disconnect each phone from the central system and reconfigure it to be part of an independent PCL system.

The computers, too, needed to be separated from a domain server located at Central and re-imaged to connect to a new independent domain connecting all the PCL computers. There were three hundred computers spread among the branches. Some were there for patron use, but many more were used by the staff to actually run the library. David explained to me that each machine took an hour to reconfigure. We were already in June, and our contract to run the libraries started on July 1st.

We also needed someone to create and run a website for the library. In that area, we were very lucky. Stephanie Shea, who worked at PPL as the website specialist in the marketing area, had been disturbed by the disparity between what PPL's publicity said about the actions of PPL in 2007 and 2008 and what Stephanie knew to be true. As soon as she learned of the creation of PCL, Stephanie contacted Patricia and asked to be part of the new library system. She was exactly what we needed. Stephanie immediately bought the domain name "provcomlib.org" for our new library and went to work building our website so it would be operational on July 1, 2009, our first day.

We also had to set up a maintenance department for PCL. With nine buildings, many of which had been neglected for years, maintenance hires turned out to be among the most crucial. At the time of the split, PPL had a maintenance department of seven people (a supervisor, a facility manager, four facility technicians, and a cleaner) in addition to contracting with an outside cleaning company to maintain and clean the Central Library and its nine branches. We only had money to hire four people to maintain the ancient plumbing and electrical systems, keep the buildings clean, plow the sidewalks and parking lots in the winter, cut the grass of those libraries which had lawns in the summer, move furniture, set up for events in the separate libraries, and even build and furnish offices that were needed. With so little money, an outside company was a non-starter for us. The problem was especially acute because maintenance of the buildings had been deferred for so many years. Four of the seven library buildings were very old: Knight Memorial had been built in 1924, Wanskuck in 1928,

Smith Hill in 1932, and Mt. Pleasant in 1949. Sad to say, the boilers and electrical systems of these buildings were not much younger.

Key to being able to deal with the situation was the hiring of Mike Nickerson, who had been a maintenance technician at PPL since 2000. He had the institutional knowledge of how the antique boilers and electrical circuits worked in these old buildings, or rather how these systems did not work. Lucky for us, Mike was interested in joining PCL. He had watched with disgust as PPL spent grant money on the downtown library, which did not need it, while the branches continued to decay.

Mike wrote a report of everything wrong with the buildings and gave it to us. Incredibly, we were still determined to keep all nine branches open. To our dismay, the concerns outlined in his report were quickly validated. Soon after PCL started operating, Alix Ogden, the mayor's representative on the board, suggested that all the buildings be examined by city inspectors to ascertain the problems clearly. The first to be examined was Mt Pleasant. Building inspectors, along with the fire marshal, arrived to check out the electrical, mechanical, and plumbing systems. The meeting quickly adjourned when the Fire Marshall, after five minutes in the building, suggested he would have to shut down the building immediately. That was scary. We did not ask for examinations of the other buildings.[1]

Mike became the head of PCL's four-person maintenance and repair department, which included PPL maintenance technicians Moses Lilly, and Louis Garcia, who only spent half of his time doing maintenance (the rest of his time he drove the van delivering books), and Frank Grinchell who did the cleaning. Sue Gibbs, our business director, took over a second job as the facilities director, raising the money needed to pay for major repairs and projects and scheduling and supervising the progress of the renovations.

---

1 Interview with Mike Nickerson November 7, 2023.

Mike told me that as soon as he was hired, his first job was to build office spaces for the administrators. In our rush to gain the contract, we had never really considered where our administration (which we wanted to keep small) would work. But Mike worked it out. Spending down some of the $50,000 I had lent PCL on needed tools and construction materials, he quickly created the new office space in Knight Memorial. Mike was so able and so unflappable in the face of the unbelievable physical challenges of our dilapidated buildings that others and I soon dubbed him the M.V.P. of PCL.

Another issue to solve was book transportation. We had never thought about the daily transportation of books necessary between libraries when you reserve a book that is not on the shelf of your local library. The Office of Library Services (OLS) transports books from other Rhode Island library systems to Providence. But we needed a van to ferry the books between the libraries within our system. And we would have to hire someone to drive this van. True to form, PPL refused to give or sell us its van even though they would no longer need to make deliveries between branches. So, one day, Patricia and I took ourselves to a U-Haul agency to check into the possibility of renting a van. We looked and felt pretty pathetic kicking the tires of the different vans. Neither of us knew a damn thing about vans. Luckily, Ray Arsenault, the President of the Mt Pleasant Friends, who was more knowledgeable, took over the job of looking into getting a van before Mike ultimately found a very old one for us.

We were still arguing with PPL over the question of what came with the branch libraries when they were "turned over." On record was Rob Taylor's statement on December 18[.] 2008, that the library was "willing to donate the branch buildings and their contents (book, computers, furnishings) to the city."[2] But PPL was now bulking on transferring the buildings to the city. They wanted the city to purchase

---

2 Philip Marcelo, "New Library Plan Would Close 5 Branches," *Providence Journal* (December 18, 2008,)

the seven buildings from them for $8 million. This was far too much for the city. Negotiations went on and on. Patricia wondered if we could actually open the libraries on July 1st as planned without settling this question. Jay advised us not to sign any contract with the city until the ownership of the buildings had been resolved. Finally, on June 30th, the city decided to sign a master lease with PPL to rent the seven library buildings and sign a sublease renting them to us in turn. The issue of who would be responsible for paying for needed repairs to the buildings was left in the air."[1] Where was that assistance now?[2]

Signing the Contract

AT LAST, EVERYTHING THAT COULD BE DONE HAD BEEN DONE. WE only had to sign the contract with the city. All the founders were very excited about finally bringing our plan to fruition. On Tuesday evening, June 30th, Marcus and I went to the city hall to sign the contract. But there was still another surprise. A good one. Unbeknownst to us, there were people in the business community who were excited about the transfer of the branches to us. As we waited to meet with the mayor, Bob Vincent, the senior vice president of corporate affairs at GTECH, came up to me. "G-Tech," he told me, "would like to give computers to PCL for children to use at each of the nine branches. We will supply the computers, monitors,

---

1 Philip Marcelo, "New Library Plan Would Close 5 Branches," *Providence Journal* (December 18, 2008,)
2 The city's lack of ownership of the buildings made it difficult for us to apply for grants to pay for desperately needed repairs. The ownership of the buildings remained a thorny issue until July 2011, when the buildings were finally transferred from PPL to the city for $5 million to be paid over five years.

and child-size desks to form separate computer pods for the kids," I was absolutely overwhelmed. I thanked him profusely. But then, worried about how our staff who had to share computers would manage to administer the libraries, I blurted out that the offer was wonderful but what we really needed was more computers for our staff. Amazingly, he answered, "Well, we can see about that." And a few months after we took over, G-Tech also gave us computers for the staff!

It was now time to sign the contract with the city to run all nine branch libraries. Signing for PCL, Marcus remarked, "Many people thought that this was an impossible task. In many other cities, libraries are facing cuts and closures. But the community here said, 'Yes, we want our libraries.' What we've created here is a model that's already gaining interest across the nation."[3] We were now in charge of Providence's community libraries. Mission accomplished!

The next morning, July 1st, was opening day, and it was pouring rain. Thank goodness our opening plans had not depended too much on outdoor celebrations as the rain fell in sheets. While the librarians and clerks, now PCL employees, checked out books at all nine libraries to waiting borrowers, the Friends Groups, founders, community politicians, and neighborhood patrons crowded in to help celebrate our new library system. After ribbon-cutting ceremonies with local officials at each library, everyone lit into rich, gooey cakes to celebrate the birth of PCL. We had planned to mark the unity of the nine libraries by having a book chosen at one branch and delivered by foot to the next branch. But the weather put an end to that plan, except for one book which I seem to remember

---

3 Philip Marcelo, "City's branch libraries go their own way," Providence Journal (July 1, 2009).

was transported from one branch to its neighboring branch courtesy of the Providence police.[1]

The next morning, our libraries opened as usual. Patrons came in and found their favorite clerks and librarians there, ready to help them. The transaction was very smooth. In fact, the transfer was so smooth that it took years for the general public to realize that a new library, one that had been created originally to save five branch libraries from being destroyed, was now providing library services for the entire city of Providence. But then, that's how it should have worked. And it did.

---

1 The project of delivering a special book to a neighboring library to show the unity of the system was carried out the following year on our first anniversary when, thankfully, it wasn't raining.

Ribbon cutting at Smith Hill Library on opening day.

Ribbon cutting at Wanskuck Library on opening day with Councilman Mancini and Patricia Raub.

Epilogue

When you are in the middle of something and determined to succeed, you don't always realize how crazy it is. You, or at least I, are just hell-bent on getting through it and accomplishing the goal. It is only now, in writing this book, that I realize how improbable our chance of succeeding was—of either forcing PPL to reform itself and keep the nine libraries open or of convincing the city that the best way to provide library service for the people of Providence was to go with us, a truly untried and inexperienced new corporation. We created PCL because we just wanted to save five neighborhood branches, mostly in low-income areas that were being jettisoned by PPL. We discovered on July 1, 2009, that we were now running the largest library system in Rhode Island. Fifteen years have passed since PCL took over the libraries. Although there have been some tough moments, and it took all of the skills and connections of our very able chief operating officer, Sue Gibbs, to keep us from going into the red, there was never a moment that PCL ever threatened to close down any of its nine libraries.

You will be happy to know that, over time, PCL has been able to bring our buildings up to code. When you come to a community library, you no longer are in danger of tripping over a bucket set out to catch rainwater. Nor do you have to worry that you will be caught in an undetected fire. Slowly, over the years, the libraries were

Preparing balloons at Fox Point on opening day.

Linda Kushner at Fox Point on opening day

Ribbon cutting in the rain at Olneyville Library on opening day

Marcus Mitchell celebrating opening day at Olneyville Library

brought up to standards. We no longer had to hold our breath when the fire marshall visited.

Between 2012 and 2021, the structural problems of the libraries were systematically corrected. Starting with Smith Hill in 2012, soon after the building was transferred to the city, the exterior was completely redone, a new roof was installed, the walls were repainted, new windows were installed, and the gutters were repaired. After that, the interior was refurbished, and an air conditioning system was installed so the library could be used comfortably during the summer months.

Next, PCL went to work on the Wanskuck Library. In 2016, it got a new roof, and the walls were repainted. A new fire protection system was installed. Fittingly, the Washington Park Library, which was housed in an old firehouse, had its alarm system brought up to code. Mt Pleasant, the library that the fire Marshall had threatened to shut down in 2009, was also brought up to code.

The library that was hardest to bring up to safety standards was Knight Memorial. This was in part because it is so immense (with three floors of stacks below the main floor). But it was also because its boiler and electric system were so antiquated. But by 2021, the needed repairs, replacements had been made, and a new fire alarm system was finally completed, along with major electrical upgrades.

All of this was possible because Sue Gibbs kept a sharp eye out for grants available for capital improvements. During this period, she raised over $6,000,000 in grants from the Champlin Foundation, HUD Community Development Block Grants, and occasional gifts from individuals.

Inside the libraries, there was a real revolution. Gone was the time when a trip to the library meant a quiet visit to choose a book to take out. Coming to the library now was an adventure! From the start, we had known that we wanted our libraries to be interactive spaces where users of all ages were encouraged to become involved in learning through doing and where the library was a space for the

GED grads. 2023 Knight Memorial Library

community to advance their interests. We succeeded beyond our wildest dreams when we hired Michelle Novello as our program director. Michelle scoured the city for programs and activities she thought would be exciting for the communities. She then made it a point to bring the activity to the community library. Our libraries now became centers for arts, games, learning, and celebrations. Whether you chose to do origami, perform hip-hop poetry, watch ballet maybe for the first time, or be a CyberKid learning how to build a computer, new worlds opened up for you when you came to the library.

Michelle suggested that we focus on two groups who particularly needed the support of the library: children from low-income homes and Latinx adults. Research showed that children from low-income homes in Providence, who often lacked books in the home and access to programs that middle-class families take for granted, suffered enormous learning loss over the summer. She obtained a $350,000

Child and mother at "Family Night" Olneyville Library

"Ready for Kindergarten" federal grant for PCL to allow the libraries to offer fun programs to prepare kids who had not had the benefit of books in the house and/or preschool for entering school. She also initiated the summer reading program to fight summer learning loss. Here, librarians, working together with Providence teachers, established the list of books to be read. Then PCL made sure that not only were the books available at the community libraries but that there was a summer program complete with prizes to ensure maximum participation.

Another big change in the libraries was to bring the Latinx community to the center of the library. According to the 2010 census, 38.1% of Providence's residents were of Latinx descent. Michelle Novello and Carolina Briones, PCL's bi-lingual outreach specialist, with the continuous input of leaders of the Latinx community, created myriads of programs to address the needs of the Latinx

Story Hour 2017. Olneyville Library

"Growth with Google" (Learning Google apps.) Smith Hill Library

community.[1] First, using a crew of twenty-five volunteer tutors, they set up ESL (English as a second language) classes, which immediately filled up. Then, they created a Spanish language GED (high school equivalency) class. In its first year, twelve people graduated from the Spanish GED program and went on to take their GED high school tests. The next year, fifty-one students graduated. Through 2020, 746 people completed their GED programs at PCL. These courses were augmented by computer and citizenship classes in Spanish. During Hispanic Heritage Month (September 15 to October 15), Knight Memorial and South Providence became the sites of cultural celebrations. Perhaps the most ambitious event, a brainchild of Carolina's, was the very successful Spanish language book fair first held at the South Providence library in 2015.

But the library served the needs of the entire, diverse community. So, after so many years of teaching Spanish-speaking people to speak English, PCL introduced Spanish classes for English speakers! Everyone was served.

You will also be happy to know that the rancor and anger that accompanied the library reformers' attempts to reform PPL so that it was responsive to the community needs and then ultimately, in 2009, to create PCL to maintain the nine branches, began to subside when PPL finally transferred the buildings to the city in 2012. With the retirement of Dale Thompson in 2014 and the hiring of Jack Martin as PPL's Executive Director, things took a great leap forward. Today, Jack and Cheryl Space, the Director of the Community Libraries of Providence (formerly PCL), meet regularly to ensure that the two library systems work together to fill the needs of all the residents of Providence.

---

1 Michelle and Carolina created "Bienvenidos Latinos," composed of a group of 20 leaders of the Hispanic community with whom they met twice a year to hear their ideas for new programs and hear their critiques of ongoing programs.

When I think about all the work that was involved in creating PCL and the great doubt at that time that it would endure, I take comfort in the fact that for fifteen years, an entire generation of Providence school children has been able to rely on their neighborhood libraries to be there to help them with schoolwork. They have been there as a place to go to chill out at afternoon clubs and activities. This has made the fight we had to create PCL very worthwhile indeed.

Building a computer. 2017. Mt. Pleasant Library

This computer was built by
Edison Ramos
and
Jimmy Torres
April 2017

A completed computer. 2017. Olneyville Library

Big Nazo Comic Fest. 2019. Mt Pleasant

Chess club. 2016. Washington Park Library

Cheryl Space, Director of the Community Libraries,
leading the 13th anniversary of the community libraries at PVD Fest

Acknowledgments

The historian Ruth Morganthal once asked me when I was a member of the Rhode Island General Assembly if I was interested in writing a book about my legislative experience. I answered her, I'm afraid, rather flippantly, "I write laws, not books." In a way, it was similar with the creation of PCL. At many points during the struggle, someone in our group would say "what we are doing is novel." "It is important." "Someone should write a book about it so it can serve as a guide for others trying to save their libraries." But we were too busy responding to the latest crisis to step back from the project and see its full dimensions. Even worse, we didn't even systematically preserve our work. I was amazed when I began to research our effort and gather notes from different people for this book to discover how frequently we failed even to date our letters and memos.

I am indebted to innumerable people who shared with me their memories and, in some cases, their notes of the events between 2004–2009 leading up to the creation of PCL. Some of them are named in the book as players who led the effort. But there are so many more individuals who shared with me their memories of marching in protests, attending meetings, and writing letters to keep the cause alive.

Even though I thought I was a central figure in this activity, I was amazed to learn how much work other people were also doing at the same time. I am particularly thankful to Elaine Heebner, who shared her two wonderfully organized giant notebooks of notes, emails, and news clippings documenting her and others' efforts.

Of course, I am indebted to Patricia Raub, the historian among us, who actually wrote a history of libraries in Providence.[1] But her scholarly work covered the entire history of libraries in Providence since 1753, not just our history. I was disappointed that our achievement had been reduced to just the latest development. I felt we deserved a whole book that explored our struggle in all its glory. So, when Patricia closed her comprehensive book with my statement about birthing a library, it struck me as a good place for me to jump in and tell our story, warts and all.

I am indebted to Patricia not only for stimulating me "to take pen in hand" but also for sharing with me all the records that she, as a historian and as the leader of the Library Reform Group, had managed to save from that period. And, of course, I am also thankful for her good advice.

This book could not have been written without the generous help of Ellen Schwartz, the financial wizard of our group. It is well known that while I can do a lot with words, numbers are beyond my ken. So, while Ellen had the job of figuring out what PPL was doing with its numbers and explaining it to the Mayor's Office, City Council, and other important actors back in 2009, she also had the additional burden of explaining it to me privately. Well, it turned out that when I set out to write this book fifteen years later, my mathematical ability

---

1 Patricia's study is divided into three parts. Part 1, "'A Bewildering Variety': The Beginning of Libraries in Providence," was published in *Rhode Island History* (Fall 2021), Volume 79, Number 1. Part 2, "Branching Out, Opening Local Libraries in Providence Neighborhoods, 1870s -1932," was published in *Rhode Island History*, Spring 2023, Volume 80, Number 2. The third part, "Saving Providence Public Library: Financial Crisis and Community Activism," has not yet been published.

had not improved. I am indebted to Ellen for making sure, once again, that the numbers are right. But even more importantly, I am grateful that Ellen was willing to sit down with me, carefully review the book, and share with me her perceptions and experiences in creating PCL.

And, of course, I am most grateful to my daughter Nina Kushner, an experienced writer and editor of historical books, who took the time from her busy schedule to proofread and edit this book, gently advising me to change cherished language for words that more clearly expressed my ideas.

Last of all, I want to thank my husband, Harold J. Kushner, himself an author of many books on mathematics, who supported not only the battle to create PCL in 2009 but this smaller effort to memorialize it.

About the Author

LINDA J. KUSHNER IS A FORMER STATE legislator and retired attorney who lives with her husband in Providence Rhode Island. Always a problem solver and social organizer, Kushner in 2004, turned her attention to the neighbor-hood libraries which were in danger of being extinguished. With a small group of reformers, she launched a five year battle garnering the support of thousands of Rhode Islanders. It ended in 2009 with the creation of a new community library system which preserved all of Providence's neighborhood libraries.